The Jon Boat Years

THE
Jon Boat
Years

And Other Stories Afield
with Fine Friends, Fair Dogs,
a Shotgun, and a Fly Rod

Jim Mize

Foreword by Jim Casada
Drawings by Bob White

THE UNIVERSITY OF
SOUTH CAROLINA PRESS

Text © 2023 Jim Mize
Foreword by Jim Casada © 2023 University of South Carolina
Drawings © 2023 Bob White

Published by the University of South Carolina Press
Columbia, South Carolina 29208

www.uscpress.com

Manufactured in the United States of America

32 31 30 29 28 27 26 25 24 23
10 9 8 7 6 5 4 3 2 1

Library of Congress Cataloging-in-Publication Data
can be found at http://catalog.loc.gov/.

ISBN: 978-1-64336-383-7 (paperback)
ISBN: 978-1-64336-384-4 (ebook)

For all those who have spent time with me afield,
laughing and creating these stories.

Bob White, *Pushing Through,* pencil on archival paper

CONTENTS

A Whiff of Skunk

The Colorado Years

Pondering Deer Stuff

In Pursuit of Bearded Birds

Of Ducks and Dogs

Upland Birds

FOREWORD

Mine was the great good fortune to grow up in a time and place where storytelling was an integral part of daily life. Whether the tales came from regulars gathered at the local liar's bench known as Loafer's Glory, my father looking back with longing on his boyhood days, a group of campers gathered around a backcountry campfire, or my beloved Grandpa Joe, they were invariably something to be cherished. Even though nothing more than a starry-eyed youngster who hung on every word of those tales, deep within my innermost being I realize they were important, a practice in oral tradition that spanned generation after generation and were worthy of perpetuation. That was particularly the case when the stories involved hunting, fishing, or life in the outdoors. Whatever modest success I have enjoyed as a writer owes a great deal to those tellers of tales from the days of what I now realize was a magical youth.

Yet while reading the stories contained in the pages of this book while simultaneously looking back to that lost world of long ago when I was growing up, realization has gradually dawned that sharing mesmerizing stories, as Jim Mize has done here, actually transcends the oral wonders woven by my Grandpa Joe and a host of other mentors, male and female, who took me to raise in my highland homeland of the Great Smokies. That's because those raconteurs from yesteryear had multiple advantages a writer such as Mize does not enjoy.

For starters, they often weren't required to take the listener vicariously to the scene. He was already there geographically speaking, and often the link from place setting to story was a palpable one. For example, when my Grandpa Joe waxed poetic, though misty-eyed, on days of hunting squirrels when gigantic American chestnuts still reigned supreme as the king of Eastern forests, we might be standing alongside a stump serving as a natural gravestone for this vanished woodland monarch. Or perhaps we would be amidst a bottomland grove of black walnut trees, gathering their nuts while my grandsire mused about the tree's wood and its uses (he called walnuts "three generation" trees because it takes that long for one to reach timbering maturity).

Along with surroundings serving as a backdrop to stories, those who were the tellers of tales enjoyed the significant advantage of being able to use various body motions—a waving of hands, shuffling of feet, or maybe a finger pointing heavenward to remind the listener of a fast-fleeting grouse or scudding snow clouds serving as harbingers of a winter storm—for visual support. Had you tied my Grandpa Joe's hands and restrained him in the rocking chair that served as his throne when he was in full rhetorical flight, he would have been rendered speechless. He simply was unable to share any of his many chronicles of outdoor adventures without his hands. While Grandpa wasn't exactly a magsman, embellishing was a part of his stock in trade, and in that regard, gesticulations rivaled his verbiage in terms of importance. Add to that the fact that mere physical presence adds to the magnetism of any gifted storyteller, and realization readily dawns that anyone who can weave a tempting, titillating tapestry exclusively through use of the written word is an individual of rare talent.

I'm not talking about straightforward hook-and-bullet accounts laden with product promotion and hero worship that sadly form the hallmark of much of what passes for storytelling in today's outdoor print media. Instead, in my personal view what constitutes truly endearing and enduring outdoor literature comes from offerings that harken back to the genius of giants of the genre writers such as Robert Ruark, Nash Buckingham, Caroline Gordon, Havilah Babcock, Gene Hill, Gordon MacQuarrie, and Archibald Rutledge. Jim Mize is a contemporary throwback to those sporting scribes of yesteryear and a worthy successor to them and their craft.

Although arguably best known as a humor writer, a genre where he has shown true mastery (and one that is devilishly difficult to offer with anything approaching consistent appeal), Mize is far more than a one-trick pony. The forty-odd tales in this work leave no doubt in that regard. The author shows real feel for the type of tales that tug at readers' hearts, and knowingly or otherwise he demonstrates the truism that often the finest writing on the outdoors results from personal passions of the author. If you can read some of these pieces, such as those involving Mize's advice to his grandchildren, his affinity for deeply meaningful moments from a lifetime of sport, or reflections on simple treasures all of us accumulate over the course of decades devoted to the world of the wilds and not be moved, let me offer some well-intentioned advice and a general thought.

Should the stories offered here fail to affect your emotions or stir your imagination—maybe bringing misty eyes, a quiet chuckle, or a wry smile as you are reminded of a similar situation in your own life—you need to make haste to schedule the next available appointment with a local shrink. You've got a hole in your soul and the gears of your outlook on life are grinding badly. On a far more positive note, I don't think this is likely to be the case. Instead, as you delve into this work, moving seamlessly from one delightful tale to the next (they are grouped loosely in sections, but in truth each story stands staunchly on its own), methinks you will discover a heady mix of wit, whimsy, wisdom, and wonderment.

The Jon Boat Years is a striking example of what used to be called a "read" book or bedside companion. It's a work for a restful hour beside a cheery fire on a winter's evening or perched on a porch rocking chair while a summer shower hammers on a tin roof overhead. You move from one little gem to the next like the flow of a gentle run in a trout stream. At one moment you are enthralled and then, transitioning to another tale, you find yourself enchanted once again. Always, though, you are deeply engrossed in what you are reading.

I have no idea whether Mize compiled this work with an underlying concept that it would constitute a book of the "best of" genre, but certainly there are selections aplenty that demonstrate he ranks in the highest echelons of today's outdoor writers. Several stories will lay a firm hold on a corner of one's soul, and time and again readers will find themselves nodding in agreement or, and this is of supreme importance, realizing that Jim Mize has just laid bare the glories of the outdoor experience. In doing so Mize brings what all of us who hunt, fish, or wander along amidst the wonders of nature fully realize yet find almost impossible to express. We know we are amidst a magical realm; we just can't convey that sense wonder to others. Jim Mize can, however, and in his ability to capture the elusive essence of sport, he serves as a voice for all of us. That's a rare gift and is precisely what makes *The Jon Boat Years* a treasure that should be read and enjoyed not just now but for generations to come.

Jim Casada
AUGUST 2022

PREFACE

Through the years, I've viewed time spent outdoors much as Havilah Babcock did when he wrote in *The Deacon's Grandpa*: "Time is not something to be saved. It's something to be spent." This book is a tribute to that spirit.

The stories in this book are interlaced with humor. Time outdoors is often filled with laughter, quiet contemplation, and wonder. The tales in this book reflect all those emotions.

The world outdoors is also a place to share with those you care about. Old friends, youngsters, family, and pups gather to make memories outdoors. Bonds are made that last a lifetime.

These stories are grouped by topic, so if you have a favorite pursuit, you can read ahead. Perhaps you will even want to come back to them from time to time.

Hopefully, you will find encouragement in these words and do as Babcock suggests, not to save time but to make sure it is well spent.

Across Generations

Passing the baton across generations can
be as simple as handing down a fly rod or
sharing wisdom about a good pup.

Bob White, *First Fish,* pencil on archival paper

First Pup

The man sat on the top step below the porch, his hair silver like the tin roof that shaded him. In the yard, a Lab pup chased a sandy-haired boy around in circles. The pup, so black he could have been his own shadow, looked all floppy ears and big feet, a promise of the dog to come. After a bit, the boy lay down in the grass and let the pup pounce on his stomach.

The man watched them play until the boy's eyes fell on him.

"You know," said the man, "that pup's like a toy now, but someday he's going to become a dog. What you do with him between now and then determines what kind of dog you'll have."

The boy looked at the pup nestled on his belly and imagined him fully grown. He then looked at the man and said, "What do I need to do?"

The man saw in the boy's expression that he was listening, so he spoke from his heart rather than his head.

"Seems to me you only need to know two things to raise a good dog."

The man sat quietly, letting this sink in. He continued after the boy asked, "And what are they?"

"First," the man started, "you need to understand that this dog thinks he's taking care of you. You're the most important person in the world to him. A good dog will lay down his life for you. He'd step between you and a bear, jump into a flood after you fell in, and keep watch over you while you sleep."

The boy took another look at the pup while the old man continued.

"When you go to school, that pup will be waiting for you to come home. When you go to the woods, that pup will go along to keep an eye on you. When he runs through the trees and looks back, he's checking up on you. If he loses you for a bit, he'll get anxious till he finds you again. When you are both in a room, he's going to lie down beside you. There's no dishonesty in a dog. Mischief, maybe, curiosity surely, but he does it because he wants to be with you. So you need to know that you're the most important person in the world to this pup and not take it for granted."

The pup, worn out from play, dozed on the boy's stomach. The boy's hands balanced him there to keep him from rolling off. A little softer now, as if not wanting to wake the pup, the boy asked, "And what's the second thing?"

The man brushed his calloused hands together as if he were dusting off dirt after working. He let his thoughts line up in his mind, so they came out just right.

"All the while he thinks he's taking care of you, you are really taking care of him. He's already told you that you're the most important person in the world to him. You need to honor that."

"How, Gramps?"

"Well, with little things. When you wake up hungry in the morning, he's hungry, too. Make sure he eats before you do. When he gets uncomfortable and needs to go outside, you take him. When it gets cold out and his water bowl freezes into a block, you've got to thaw it [out] so he isn't thirsty. And when night comes, he needs a warm place to sleep. He'd do the same and more for you if he could.

"Remember too that there's nothing in a dog you don't put in him."

The boy's eyebrows tilted up inquisitively, so the man continued before he asked.

"What I mean is that between now and him becoming a dog you need to teach him what's important and do it in the right way. Dogs reflect their owners. You put goodwill into a dog and he's going to be a good dog. You take out your anger and frustration on him and you'll reap what you sow."

The man kept his eyes on the boy and made sure he was listening before going on.

"You can save a dog's life with what you teach him. For instance, the dog needs to be under your direction. If he takes off into the road after a ball and a car is coming, you need to be able to stop him with a stern 'whoa' command. You don't want him jumping on people, so he needs to learn to sit. When he tries to cheat on you by creeping when told to whoa—and he will—don't let him. A little bit wrong is still wrong. No one likes to be told what to do, not even a dog. But sometimes it's important enough you have to train them to obey.

"After that, you can teach him tricks or hunting commands, but first you need him to know the things that will keep him safe. And you need to teach him these things without losing your temper. Lay a hand on the dog and he'll start to avoid your hand. That's not what you want. You want him to do the right things because he wants to please you. And he will."

The man grew quiet and just enjoyed watching the two on the grass, each content to be with each other. The summer afternoon seemed to pause; no wind blew, and it was hard to detect the shadows' creep. The boy and the pup both seemed to sleep.

After a bit, the boy spoke as if the conversation had continued without a break.

"That's a lot."

The man grinned to himself knowing the message had been delivered.

"It is," he agreed. "The good news is that you don't have to do it all at once. You just need to do it all the time."

The boy nodded and the afternoon grew quiet again. The man thought to himself that this had been a good day. When three individuals can be good company without a word being spoken, that's a good day. When something important from the heart can be said and heard, that's a good day. And when you can see into the future and know that a boy and a dog would be there to take care of each other, that's a good day.

And for sure, that pup was going to be a fine dog.

Your Day
Will Come

My approach to fishing was inherited and likely stems from a game of chess.

Shortly after the Second World War, Dad came home, got a machinist certification, and went to work in a shop that rewired burnt-out motors for the furniture factories. Most of the guys were veterans and they brought home the habit of decorating the shop with pinup calendars. Names like Ava Gardner and Jayne Mansfield entered my vocabulary. It was an educational shop for a youngster lucky enough to hang out with a crusty old bunch of veterans.

Someone in the shop decided that they should start playing chess, so a handful of them bought chess sets and played during lunch. Dad liked it well enough that he decided he needed a sparring partner at home to sharpen his game, so he taught me. His philosophy in all competitions was that you never let your opponent win. The idea of letting a kid win to build his ego was as foreign as hunting quail with cats. This just made me try harder as the size of the prize grew with each loss.

My cousin also picked up the game, so we spent many summer afternoons lying on cool porch floors playing chess. We soon learned each other's tricks and the games were often decided by a pawn.

After a year of playing the family, I went with Dad down to the shop and he got me a game with one of the guys. My opponent probably figured I was a charity case until the sixth move when I pronounced checkmate.

I was seven years old at the time.

All the onlookers laughed so hard it embarrassed the guy and he wouldn't play me again. None of the others wanted to take the risk, so Dad and I went back to playing each other after dinner. I won occasionally, but I was approaching ten before I started playing him close to even.

Our competitions spilled over into the boat, and we kept a meticulous count of our fish. Each of us always figured out how to have bragging rights over something by the end of the day.

"I caught more than you."

"Yeah, but I had the biggest one."

"Ok, but carp don't count."

"Sure they do. They're fish, aren't they?"

"All right, but you eat yours and I'll eat mine."

Then he'd start laughing that wheezy laugh that sounded like the bear on the Saturday-morning cartoons.

By the time I was twelve, our competitions had gone from daily to seasonal. I kept a poster board on my bedroom wall with a running tally of each trip, recording only our catches of trout. The deep mountain lake we fished had a strong population of rainbows and browns, as did the tailrace that spilled out from the dam with forty-seven-degree water.

The one area of fishing that I routinely thumped him at was stream fishing for trout in that tailrace. I'd picked up a fly rod early on and lived on the river in the summers. Not only did my cousin and I know where all the big browns hid, we knew their names.

After fishing early on hot mornings, we'd wade the river looking for lures that fishermen had lost, and we routinely restocked our tackle boxes with them. On one July afternoon, I waded in over waist-deep to look behind a boulder for lures. On the bottom, a giant tail of a brown stuck out from under the rock and was as big around as my wrist just in front of his tail. Since the warden had a cabin close to this hole, this became "The Warden's Trout."

Any time we saw a large trout that refused to bite or managed to get away, we named it. Sometimes, it was referred to by the name of the hole, as in "The Cornfield Brown." Other times, the name had personality, like "The Plug Buster" or "Old Stumpy." But once he was named, we could talk in code about the fish and felt some ownership of him, as if we were destined to catch him but it just hadn't happened yet.

When my kids were growing up, my dad's philosophy of competition had worn off on me. If they wanted to win, they had to beat me. The competition was friendly, but we all knew they were going to have to earn it.

The first sport one of them took me in was basketball. By then, I'd lost a step and my son had found it, so he started getting revenge on our driveway court at twelve.

Next to go was my dominance in the dove field. By the time my son was thirteen, I noticed he had outgrown his youth model Remington, so I handed him my sixteen-gauge Winchester pump. The first time it met his shoulder the two of them fell in love. On opening day of the season that year, we shot even. On the following opening day, at fourteen, he limited out before I did. I was fading fast. My last stronghold was fly fishing for trout.

I should have seen it coming, but my daughter snuck up on me. She started by asking for a fly rod on her thirteenth birthday. We were vacationing in Maine that year and had detoured over to L. L. Bean and she picked one out. No dad in his right mind would have turned down a request like that. It was a welcome event after those early years putting Barbie's Playhouse together on Christmas Eve. You know the ones. The box proclaims it contains over one thousand pieces, like that's a good thing.

We made regular trips to the lake to practice on bluegill beds with poppers. When she went off to college, we would occasionally pick a lake halfway and meet to fish. She knew how to handle a rod.

My dominion remained the trout stream. I kept playing with fly patterns and, in fairness, made sure she had all my best patterns in her pack. But along the way she started closing the gap. I could blame it on her fishing a lot with her husband or maybe on lessons she learned fishing with guides out west. Last year though, the inevitable happened. She got in a rhythm and soundly beat me. She didn't say much about it, but her grin on the ride home said everything.

My last holdout in trout skills was with big fish. She could get me in numbers, but I consoled myself knowing that on most trips I had the biggest fish. It was a refuge my ego hid within. Browns, brooks, and rainbows . . . I cornered the market on the biggest ones.

Until this year.

This spring, we fished together even though she was seven months pregnant. I tried to convince her she had to divide her catch in two but getting beaten by both a mom and a preborn wouldn't have been much better.

So as we fished and I watched her rod tip dance with each take, I heard her reel start to spin and looked up as a twenty-inch rainbow sped by. She played it into the net, and I took her picture, documenting that my day had finally come. The domain I had owned fishing against my dad and kids now belonged to her.

I've already decided both my grandkids will be fly-fishing prodigies. On the opposite side of the family, they will be third-generation fly-fishers. On my side, they will be fourth-generation fly-fishers. Their middle names are appropriately shared with trout streams. The oldest, almost three, has already caught bluegill on his SpongeBob fishing rod and has had a practice session in the yard with a fly-rod tip and yarn.

So, to my fly-fishing daughter, I'll just say this:

Those two grandkids are going to get flies for Christmas, my best patterns. I'm going to give them little nets and show them what stonefly nymphs look like. They will be reading water by the time they are six and understand the importance of stealth in approaching wild trout. Every fishing trick I've learned over the years, I'm going to teach them. I'm telling you all of this so you know in advance.

Your day will come.

Kids Do Say
the Darndest
Things

I'm just old enough to remember Art Linkletter's show where he could entertain the world by getting kids to say what they shouldn't in ways that made us laugh. Reading an old collection of dog stories called *Cold Noses and Warm Hearts*, I happened upon a chapter by Art Linkletter relating some of the funny things that kids say about dogs.

Art had written a story one child had shared with him in an interview. Apparently the four-year-old had cried when a large friendly dog bounded up and licked him. According to Art, the exchange between mother and son went like this:

"What is it, darling?" cried his mother. "Did he bite you?"

"No," came the reply. "But he tasted me."

Children's observational skills are unfiltered and the thoughts that enter their minds exit through their mouths. The clarity of their insights often provides us with a chuckle.

A few years back, I was part of just such a kid experience on a trout stream one warm day. Usually, I can get into the stream early enough to beat the swimmers and rafters, picking up a few fish before they show up. But once the temperatures rise enough to make the trout uncomfortable, swimmers, rafters, and retrieving dogs converge on good trout water as if a carnival came to town. This is especially true below a dam where power generation releases cool water that appeals to swimmers and fish alike.

I had already been fishing a couple hours as the sun drifted higher, and temperatures rose. Knowing I had minutes left to fish, I concentrated on making a few last casts before company arrived.

The tube hatch broke out moments later, signaling it was time for me to quit. Among the first to float down were a mother and two sons. The boys looked to be about ten and five years old and were clearly enjoying their expedition. They splashed back and forth as brothers should on a warm day in a cool stream. Their focus was more on making sure the other was wet than navigating the stream.

Distracted by their frivolity, they hadn't noticed me, and they floated through the water I had just cast to. Once they saw me, while trying to move out of my way they splashed even more, putting down any fish with half a brain. These fish probably had a whole brain, as the bite had been slow and I had been outwitted.

I took this disruption as a sign to quit for the day and flipped my line out of their paths.

About then, the oldest boy exclaimed, "Look Mom, he's fly fishing."

To which the youngest responded, "You mean he's fishing for flies?"

We all had a laugh as the youngest got a brief explanation of the goal of fly fishing. If you must concede your stream to frolickers, it's better when they bring a sense of humor on their trip or at least contribute to the use of yours.

I looked over my shoulder for Art Linkletter. He would have smiled.

The Jon Boat
Years

The first boat I owned was a jon boat; I bought it over a sack lunch from a coworker at a Corps of Engineers lake, where I worked during my summers off from college. Twelve feet long, it was a stubby, square-nosed aluminum boat and came with a dented three-horse-power Eska outboard and a clamp-on electric motor. The whole rig cost me seventy-five dollars, which hints at how long ago this transaction occurred.

For the seller, the money meant buying new archery equipment for the coming fall. For me, the boat meant a level of freedom in fishing that only a jon boat can bring.

I had a 1967 Mustang back then and I fitted it with roof racks. I could slide the boat onto the roof by standing it on end and slowly leaning it until the bow hit a rack. Then I simply lifted the boat from the stern and slid it forward. Once on top, I tied the boat off on each bumper, threw straps over the middle, and carried the rest of my gear in the trunk.

With the small outboard's limited range, I always tried to put in close to where I fished. While working at the lake, I learned every road and fire trail that ran to the water, so this was no problem. To launch, I merely took the boat off the car, filled it with my gear, and then dragged it to the water by the two handles on the stern. The whole process took only a few minutes.

You might think not having any sophisticated electronics could be a handicap. But growing up on a lake you learn more about its structure than you realize. All those years of getting lures hung taught me where the submerged trees were. The nights of pulling up an anchor by hand helped me locate the deep holes and creek channels. All I missed were the blips of fish on a screen but watching for other signs filled in the blanks.

Schools of shad often dimpled the lake surface, so when I trolled, I swung around them dragging my lures through the middle going from school to school. Usually, the fish weren't far away. Also, bass rarely feed quietly in the shallows so when water blew up it could only be one thing. Instead of staring at a screen, I merely watched the water.

And I caught fish.

I worked the campgrounds on weekends, so my days off generally came during the week. That was fine by me as a quiet lake better served the needs of a small boat.

One June morning, I put in by the dam to troll the deep water for trout. I clamped rod holders on either side of the boat for two rods. On one side I ran lead line on a saltwater Penn reel. On the other, I fished a Mitchell 300 with a deep-running crankbait. The two lines ran different depths so they could pass each other on turns and never tangle.

The outboard was old when I got it and now would qualify for a fishing museum. It never held the same speed for various reasons. If trash or condensation got in the gas it would sputter to a halt and my lead line would sink while the floating crankbait rose. Usually, I could start the motor and get moving again before the lead line hit bottom.

When the motor got low on gas it would speed up, cut out, and speed up again. The gas tank was small, and I generally had to refill it once or twice a day when I stayed on the water.

The trout seemed to like the erratic movement of my baits that resulted from the inconsistent outboard. That morning as it was getting late enough to feel warm, I was trolling through a deep section of the main channel. I had been following a shaded bank that dropped sharply into the lake until I made a ninety-degree turn back toward the middle. Just as my lines curved the outboard died.

It took a few pulls, plus some muttering that always seemed to help, and as my lines went slack the motor caught. It caused the boat to jump, and my lines popped back into action. The rod with the lead line bowed, and a rainbow went airborne back toward the bank.

I cut the motor and played the fish. My lead line always lagged behind the location of the fish so I kept my eyes ahead to guess where it would jump next. Leaping and fighting in the warm water at the surface finally exhausted the trout and I slid it into my net, a fat four-pound rainbow. From a hefty diet of shad, the fish had developed a sagging belly and a bright pink stripe. By local standards, this was a fine fish.

The electric motor came into play when the bluegill spawned. Bluegill have a habit of spawning in the same vicinities every year; I had learned a few of these places scattered around the lake. When I wanted a good mess of fish, that's where I headed.

Since these beds were distributed around the lake, I often drove in on fire roads or slid the jon boat in at different entry points up the lake to get close. That outboard would have gotten me there, but I didn't want to grow old while it did.

One long cove had several beds in it not far apart. I could put in half-way up the lake, run around a point and turn west, and then go a mile and I would be on the first bed.

Usually, I would use the electric motor to ease down the bank until I could see the pockmarked bottom resembling craters on the moon. Then I'd drop a mushroom anchor on a nylon rope and tie it off on the stern.

Fishing for bluegill on their beds is more fun than a washtub full of puppies. My usual approach was to cast a small foam spider over the bed and just let it sit. Before long, a thick-shouldered bluegill would rise and smack his lips on the bug.

At that point, I'd set the hook and watch the bluegill dart, shimmy, and angle away from the boat. The chunky ones went in the cooler for supper.

When you spend your workdays in the woods lunching on Beanie Weenies, a fried-bluegill supper qualifies as fine dining. I'd fillet the largest ones, dip them in a slurry of eggs and milk, and then roll them in a powder of cornmeal, flour, salt, and pepper. When the fillets hit the grease, they would sputter until they turned golden brown. Then I'd serve them with hushpuppies and baked beans, dipping the fish in cocktail sauce like fried shrimp. To this day, the memory of those dinners makes me hungry.

After catching what seemed to be the volunteers off a bed, I'd move on to the next one. Whether it was right or wrong, I believed that the secret to having them back next year in the same spot was to leave a spawning population.

When fall came, that jon boat went back to college with me. I floated rivers in it chasing smallmouth and dragged it to farm ponds for panfish.

Freedom comes in many forms. Mine was made of aluminum and cost seventy-five dollars. The old outboard made me appreciate the days it ran and taught me some new vocabulary when it didn't.

That boat followed me on every move for decades, even when I replaced it with something bigger and more reliable that I pulled on a trailer. Then one day my wife said she knew a teenage boy who needed a boat. I thought about it just for a second and said he could have it.

Freedom like that needs to be passed on.

Another Letter
to a Grandson

My library contains many books from my favorite writers, often colorful gents who wrote what was on their minds. I noticed an old library copy I'd picked up at a fundraiser, a collection of Corey Ford's work, and it had a Post-It Note marking one of the stories. I couldn't remember why I'd marked it, so I looked.

Should you be too young to remember, Corey Ford wrote the "Lower Forty" columns where an assortment of characters would assemble around a jug in Uncle Perk's store to share their semblance of wisdom.

Upon opening the book, I saw the piece I'd marked was titled "Letter to a Grandson." In it, Judge Parker and the boys had gathered at Uncle Perk's store to celebrate the birth of the judge's grandson by passing a jug of Old Stump Blower. While they commemorated the addition of another hunter and fisherman to the family, they realized the boy would never hunt over the judge's favorite bird dog, now up in years. In doing so, they became aware of their own mortality.

As a hedge against death, the judge left a letter to his grandson to be read by the Judge on the boy's sixteenth birthday, or if that wasn't possible, the boy was to go off alone and read the letter aloud to himself.

When I looked at the dates, it dawned on me that our grandsons were born fifty years apart almost to the day. Taking to heart the wisdom of my forefathers, particularly those who passed a jug around in a country store, I wrote my grandson this letter:

To my Grandson,
You have been blessed by being born into a family of hunters and fishermen. No doubt as both your parents hunt and fish, that part of the inheritance is assured. As you get your feet under you, the two retrievers that roam the house will be looked at as siblings with tails that flog and tongues that make you cover your face and squeal.

I have only a little advice worth passing on after all these years. First, when you get to college, skip all those courses on morality. A lot of really smart people make this harder than it should be. Just live your life like your momma's always watching. She probably will be.

Not all the stories about the family will be passed along, but there's one you might like to know that no one else will tell you. In the gun cabinet, there's an old single-barrel twelve gauge with the faint marking of a skull and crossbones on it. It's called a Wide Awake. No one ever takes it out so I doubt anyone will complain if you do. It belonged to three of your great-great uncles who carried it to the still with them when they made moonshine whiskey. This was a respectable trade back then if you made high-quality liquor, which they did.

I should add, one of them had a mean streak and was said to have put a knife in a fellow's back in a bar. Our bloodlines, however, should have diluted well before his gets to you. Just be aware of it so you keep your wits about you in heated moments.

In a couple years, you will face a decision on whether to go straight to college or join a military service. Let me just say that this is your decision so don't let anyone make it for you. It will shape the rest of your life. I will only add that our family has already invested blood and life defending this country. Having traveled all over this world, the main thing I have learned is that this country is worth defending. So you can either follow in their footsteps or find another way to protect what's worth protecting.

The world was a bigger place when I came into it. If a fellow could hunt and fish, he could at least feed himself. I've wagered at times on my fishing luck that I'd not go hungry sleeping under the stars and the fish found their way into hot butter.

Your world is shrinking. I would encourage you to recognize that it can no longer take care of you without you in turn taking care of it.

I'll leave you a few tools of our avocation, but know that it's what's in your head that makes them effective. These belongings are mostly just excuses to have a November wind cut through your collar, a campfire that warms you in the front while your backside freezes, or the chance to wade wet on a cool mountain stream on a hot July afternoon.

To start with, I'm leaving you a nine-foot four-weight fly rod that most of my big fish fell to. Your parents witnessed a two-foot brown I caught on a small stream, so long he sagged in the middle. Hank and

Sage were pups then and played on the bank while I watched that fish use the pool and every trick he had to get away. Let me add that no fish I ever lost was to the fault of this rod.

You should take my fly-tying gear as well, knowing that it never hurts to be on the sparse side of most patterns. You can tell by my fly boxes that I like to add features that don't come on store-bought patterns. I figure the fish have seen them already. Check my boxes and you'll see what I mean.

A few other things I've learned are worth passing along so you don't have to waste time learning them yourself.

First, never let the weatherman talk you out of a trip. The worse the weather, the better the story.

Second, never avoid a trip because you have to get up early. Watching the world wake up is a show that only plays once a day.

Last, fish each hole with the idea you have to cast where no one else thought to or worked hard enough to reach. Old fish only get that way for a reason.

So in closing, I leave you all these things as if they were mine to give. Count every friend a treasure, laugh with your dogs more than you scold them, and cherish every moment outdoors. In the end, they were too few.

As an old scribe once wrote, "I raise my glass to you across the years," in case I am not here to read this letter to you myself. Know that you made me proud and when your momma's not watching, I will be.

Your Grandfather

And as I lay down my pen, I wished heartily I could share a swig of Old Stump Blower with Judge Parker and the boys down at Uncle Perk's store.

A Letter to a Granddaughter

After penning my own letter to my grandson, I felt my task complete until my granddaughter came along. My philosophy on raising daughters is that you should treat them like kids until they realize they are girls. By then, they will fish, shoot, and treat the family retrievers like siblings.

So having penned a letter to my grandson, I felt it a slight should I not follow up with a letter to my granddaughter. I figured the boys back at Uncle Perk's store would approve. The letter went like this:

To my Granddaughter,
You have already been blessed by being born into an outdoor family. I have no doubt that the shadow of your older brother will give you shade for only a few years as you will begin to find your own way through marshes, creeks, and fields.

The advice I can share after all these years is as sparse as good friends at my age. Still, I will share what I have as the more I give away the richer I become.

You are growing up in a world where everything is possible. That doesn't mean it's all good. The difference between being a woman and a girl is knowing that difference. Even at two, you had to try everything. If someone told you a pan was hot, you had to touch it. The Bible says, "Test everything, hold fast what is good." That doesn't mean try everything, but instead, weigh it, consider it, and let all the bad things pass.

Your outdoor roots run deep. Your great-grandmother could handle a boat and light matches with a .22 rifle. When your great-grandfather took up taxidermy, it was your great-grandmother who painted life into those fish.

The women in the family who lived before you spent late evenings on the water with their families, listening to the soft roar of a Coleman lantern while rods slowly bobbed over the side of a boat rocking in the breeze.

They went outside at night to hear whip-poor-wills and screech owls. When given the choice of places to live, these women preferred the remote areas where bears passed through their yards and bobcats might spend a cold night in an abandoned shed.

And they encouraged the kids they raised to value those moments outdoors above others whether splashing barefoot in a creek chasing salamanders or wading waist-deep behind a seine catching crappie minnows.

You have already taken ownership of the two family retrievers, referring to them as "my dogs." You have embraced tents and campfires, sleeping bags, and toasted marshmallows. If there is a rock to climb, you are usually soon found at its top.

When you see your mom with an armload of fishing gear about to make an afternoon excursion to a trout stream, you test the waters to see if you can tag along. And you continue to ask before each trip, knowing one day the answer will be "yes."

The love of the outdoors is already in you, so I have no doubt you will follow the family tradition.

I wish I could guide you through all the issues women face in the modern world, but being a man and at least two generations out of step, I realize I would probably get it wrong. So I will say only that as you lay there as a toddler, eyes wide, you have no equal so I don't expect you to come down to anyone else's level.

I have often seen young ladies handling fly rods better than their male counterparts, largely because it is finesse and not power that lights a small fly with a dimple over a trout's nose. I have a three-weight fly rod that will dance in your hands. It is short enough to reach under branches and flexes perfectly to respond to a strike. Take it to the high places where the speckled trout live. It is yours.

As I get older and supposedly wiser, I discovered that much of what I learned wasn't that useful in the end and the simpler the truth the more valuable it was.

For instance, choose your friends carefully. They reflect upon you and influence your path. Pick the ones that keep your feet where they belong. You'll know the difference.

Second, don't let anyone else define you. I can only imagine the world you face. Don't let them put you in a category. You are unique so live your own life.

Third, that little fly rod was made for creeks where there is no trail. Make your own. Don't be afraid to go your own way. Most of the time any fear you feel turns out worse than any of the outcomes.

So in closing, I wish I could give you half what you've given me. If I could reach across ages, I'd have you fish with the women who went before you and hear those old Coleman lanterns purr to the night sounds of cicadas and screech owls.

I'd have you backpack onto mountain tops and stare at multitudes of stars so you would remember both how small we are and how special.

I toast along with an old scribe who wrote, "I raise my glass to you across the years." I may not be here to read this letter myself so I will look upon you as one of those twinkling jewels in the sky.

Know that you made me smile as only the good things in the world can.

Your Grandfather

Once again, as I lay down my pen, I raise a toast to those boys with Judge Parker down at Uncle Perk's store and to a granddaughter who is still just a promise of a life well lived.

Fishing
with Others

The problem concerning fishing with others
is that you always have a witness.

Bob White, *Fishing Buddies,* pencil on archival paper

If a Tree Falls

My daughter suggested that we go fishing on Father's Day. Never one to shun a good idea, particularly one that involves fishing, I suggested we try Humility Creek and an early start.

The temperatures had hung in the nineties all week; even darkness brought less relief than usual. The water levels were falling into that summer patter where riffles go from bouncing to gurgling. Even the woods sounded lethargic, woodpeckers spacing out their drilling into single half-hearted taps. Humility Creek warned us early that it would live up to its name.

Humility Creek falls through the North Carolina mountains in a watershed that up until now protected it with shade for cooler temperatures and stable soil for clear water even in runoff. I say up until now as an onslaught of woolly adelgids has been feasting upon the hemlocks that provided much of that shade and stability. If science has a cure for such ravenous insects, it's been a day late and a dollar short. The primary role of the hemlocks, a forest that has become a standing graveyard, now seemed to be extending their bony branches to wrap up an errant backcast.

We waded into a long, straight pool, my daughter working the riffles with a soft hackle, while I lofted a hopper into the shadows in deeper water where browns lurked. In the windless heat of the morning, a sharp crack interrupted the tranquility. I instantly recognized this sound.

Going back a few decades, I had been a forester and just getting out of college with that degree required a timber-management class that included thinning forests and cutting pulpwood for the state, or as we called it, cheap labor. Even after college, I felled several dead trees for firewood, helping friends feed their woodstoves and keeping a few odd sticks for my camping trips.

Just as a tree falls, a loud crack signals its surrender. It's a forest sound like no other. Something in the tree just gives up, like a spine snapping.

That was the sound I heard on Humility Creek that morning. With a quick look over my shoulder, I confirmed the tree was falling directly where I fished. The hemlock, having stood dead for some time, had lost all its limbs and most of its top. Now it most closely resembled a telephone pole; without limbs to grab the live branches around it and slow its fall, the tree dropped like a bludgeon.

Having recognized the tree was coming at me, I broke into a run upstream, moving without grace, stealth, or form, knees flying high in the spray. I felt like I moved in slow motion while everything around me sped up, branches breaking like mile markers being passed as the tree rushed down.

The look on my daughter's face told several stories. Having not seen me move this fast in at least a decade, her questioning expression suggested she wondered what was chasing me. Not too long before, I'd encountered a black bear just above this hole. The commotion suggested I might have met another. In any event, she quickly concluded she might need to run too, since things that chase usually catch the one in the rear.

Before she could take off and I could get more than five steps upstream, the tree hit the water so forcefully the top exploded. As the wake subsided, splinters of wood shrapnel dotted the creek and then began to float downstream. A wave broke against my leg.

The tree had fallen across my line, so I slowly untangled it and looked around to confirm the tree hadn't jarred loose another. But no more cracks came, and the woods fell silent, even the cicadas taking a breath.

In the ensuing quiet, the next sound was surprising. Laughter broke the tension and gallows humor ruled the moment. We imagined cartoon images of me being driven neck deep into soft silt and I chuckled at comments about my running form in knee-deep water. Had a bear followed me upriver, my daughter would have been no more surprised than when a tree broke free and hit the trout stream.

I've always heard that in such moments your life will pass before you. Mine didn't. This disappointed me a bit, as there is plenty of material, and I'd like to watch some episodes again, even if they played by in a flash. Either my memory is going or there just wasn't enough time before the tree fell to replay such a long life.

But afterward, this falling-tree episode prompted another memory, one of an October morning on the Fryingpan River in Colorado. The night temperatures had dropped below freezing, pushing ice crystals up on the edges of mud puddles where I parked my car, a sign the earth moves up and down on nights and days where freezing and thawing compete.

This section of the stream cut between two ridges. On one side, the paved road paralleled the creek and ran up to the lake above; on the opposite side, a dirt road allowed fishermen room to pull off and park.

When the sun first hit the ridge in front of me, the thawing released a rock the size of a pumpkin to roll and leap down the mountainside. It kicked loose gravel and rock creating its own small landslide, bounding high as it gained speed. The rock cleared the highway and hit the guardrail with a clang that caused any living creature to turn and look.

This rock foreshadowed the boulder that an hour later would give up its perch behind me. With its heft, it rolled more surely and with measured bounces. As I tracked the sound of deep thuds and breaking brush, I felt much like an outfielder seeing a ball come off the bat, rising into the sky and beginning its descent as if it tracked me, not the other way around.

As the boulder bounded into view, finding a path between sparse pines, I realized it was coming not for me but for my rental car. Every tree that could have stopped it missed. Methodically, moving with more force than speed, the giant stone cleared the woods. With one last leap, the boulder came off the mountain and cracked into another rock large enough to check its progress, stopping yards short of where I parked. The dust settled and the quiet returned as I remembered I had not checked the insurance option on my rental car.

Near misses can add color to our experiences outdoors. Providing they miss. With enough frequency, these events can make a person feel like a magnet for disaster, when in reality they serve as reminders that the world is not a static place. Catastrophes and mishaps, great and small, make mountains into rubble and trees into sawdust. It happens whether we are there to see it or not.

From this near-miss with the tree, I learned several lessons. First, a forestry degree can save your life. The split second from crack to falling tree gave me five steps. Second, on a stream littered with standing dead hemlocks, never stop to fish on the downhill side of one. Last, I think we answered that age-old question about trees falling in the woods making a sound. My answer is that there were two: the crack of the tree and my scream as I scampered like a walrus possessed.

My Buddy's Fishing Hole

This story is different than most you will read. The others may give you directions to a famous river and point you to a fifty-mile stretch that's in every guidebook, suggesting you use one of about twenty-five flies that everyone always uses. Instead, the information here will guide you to a secret spot fished by only one fisherman I know of and will only suggest one fly. For brevity's sake, let's refer to this as Ralph's Hole.

To find Ralph's Hole, get a map and locate Farmville. Highway 48 runs south from Main Street and crosses the Green River four miles out of town. Cross the bridge and turn down the second dirt road on the right. It's half a mile after you cross the bridge. Drive to the end and park. On a weekday, try to arrive by four thirty in the afternoon since Ralph gets off work at five.

Once you park and get your gear ready, forget about the big open trail leading upriver on the left side of the road. Instead, look for an almost invisible path that starts behind that large oak on the right that you almost hit pulling in. The tree has been hiding that trail for years and that's why the hole gets so little pressure except for Ralph. All the brush by the road makes it look inaccessible.

After a short walk down the hillside, you will arrive at a long hole. This is Ralph's Hole. With all the shade from the tree canopy, you can go a little heavy on your leader. I would shorten it to eight feet and about 4X tippet, preferably fluorocarbon. No, better make it 3X, because you will be fishing a large fly. I would suggest a streamer, preferably an Olive Butt Monkey in a size two.

At the bottom of the hole, you will see a log that drops into the river at a slight angle coming off the far bank. It's an old beech that has been there many years and has lost all its branches. All that is left is the trunk. Otherwise, you couldn't get a fly near it without hanging up.

Look closely just where the trunk comes off the bank and you will see a little eddy that swirls against the bank before the water eases under the log and heads downstream. Just on the edge of the eddy, underneath the log, hides a brown trout that Ralph has been trying to catch for about three years. It likes large flies and I know Ralph has never tried a Butt Monkey, so it might just fool the old codger.

Now, when you cast, aim for the eddy and coax the streamer along the trunk in short spasms like another fish just crushed it. If that doesn't work, try letting the fly drift back under the log and give it a short jerk or two like it panicked. That should be just the ticket.

When the brown hits, keep him on your side of the log and lead him upriver. Also, be careful to guide him away from that far bank. You can't see it very well, but there's a big root about a third of the way up the hole that protrudes from the bank. The old brown likes to run behind that root to pop your leader. He's done it to Ralph twice.

So take your time and let him wear himself down as long as he stays out in the middle. The big fish tends to circle the hole, but don't let him circle too big or he'll get behind that root.

As you bring him in, hopefully you have a big net and know how to use one. Don't lunge, because he's probably saved a little kick, just in case he sees an opening. Simply glide him over the front lip of the net, drop his head, and lift.

At this point, be sure and take a good picture because the *Farmville Times* will want to run it in the Sunday Sports section. Now this next part is important and not what I normally recommend, so pay close attention.

Do not release him.

You are allowed one trophy fish per day, which means the fish must exceed eighteen inches. This old bruiser is well past that. If the fish you catch is close to eighteen inches, you've got the wrong one, so let that one go and keep fishing.

What you want to do next is drive with the fish on ice back up Highway 48 to the edge of the town. There will be a tackle shop and pub called The Rusty Hook. Go in here and weigh your fish. I'm guessing about eight pounds, give or take an ounce.

At this point the owner, a portly fellow with a limp, will offer to take your picture with the fish for his bragging board. Hold the brown well out in front of you to embellish his size. That photo will then remain on the board for all to see for years, which is the whole point.

After the photo session, take a quick peek into the bar. If the fishermen there haven't noticed your fish, it is customary to take the big ones in and show them off. Expect a few pats on the back and you will not likely have to buy a beer the rest of the night. These guys know that once you are lubricated, you are more likely to let information slip. So enjoy their camaraderie, not to mention the free beer.

If you play the information out one piece at a time, you can turn it into quite a few rounds. My recommendation is that you not only tell them what fly you used, but also exactly where you caught this behemoth. There are two reasons for this. First, you already have the biggest fish in that hole. There are not two of them. Second, you are all fishermen. They expect you to lie so nothing you say will be believed. I mean, who tells where they catch big fish, much less what they caught it on.

Now, there is a chance that one of the fishermen in the pub will switch to something exceptionally potent and begin ordering doubles for himself once he sees your fish. That would be Ralph. He alone will know that the directions, the fly, the technique you used, and how the fish fought will all be true. If you want to spice the story up a bit, throw in the part about how you were smart enough to hold the big brown away from that hidden root.

Last, I would suggest that if you ever desired to have a fish mounted, splurge on this one. It's a unique old fish that you likely will not match in your lifetime. In fact, it's the sort of fish a guy could become obsessed with, hiding it from all his partners for himself so they would only know about it because they followed him down there and hid in the woods while he fished for it.

And if Ralph should by chance read this story, let me suggest that maybe the next time you find yourself in the good fortune to be given a bottle of Dry Fly Washington Wheat Whiskey, you might reconsider sharing it with one of your normally tight-lipped fishing buddies. Those other guys who helped you knock it off in one night tend to talk down at The Rusty Hook and word gets around. Sort of the way it can get around about a fellow's secret hole with a giant trout in it.

So if it ever happens again, you might get to read another fine story about a secret fishing hole involving a pool beneath a jagged old hemlock that has been struck by lightning where another good fish has been passing the years. You know the one I'm talking about.

Not that I'm bitter or anything about the whiskey. I'm just saying you should be more careful who you drink it with. I'm just saying.

The Seabee Jacket

We met on the lake. JC and his brother sat stoically in a V-bottomed aluminum boat, sidled up against a small clump of cattails on an otherwise nondescript section of bank. A school of crappie must have noticed something we couldn't, having nestled onto beds in front of their boat.

Dad and I were trying to locate the school, trolling slowly past the two brothers who tried to act like they weren't catching fish. At times, a crappie bed can seem like buried treasure; those who know where it lies don't want to tip off anyone else.

On one of our passes, JC tried heroically to hide the bend in his ultralight rod yet was unable to since a largemouth with some heft had inhaled his small, white crappie jig. JC finally gave up the charade, we all laughed, and his brother netted an eight-pound largemouth.

We congratulated him on his catch, exchanged introductions, and he invited us to pull alongside and fish.

I was entering high school that year; JC was a senior. He, Dad, and I began to fish together. JC was a fisherman good beyond his years, possessing a knack you can't teach. When deep trolling for trout before downriggers came along, he could find the right depth by some sixth sense using nothing more than lead weights. He could judge a shoreline and tell where bass would congregate and whether they would be largemouth or smallmouth.

That summer, JC took a job as a machinist in the same tool shop as Dad. The war in Vietnam was firing up and JC got called in. When he was asked which branch he wanted to serve in, he told them he liked water and was a machinist. They put him in the Navy Seabees.

I once asked him what Seabees did. He said that whenever the enemy blew something up, if you could get to it by boat, his crew rebuilt it. I asked if it was dangerous and he said, "Not if they're gone."

I took his hint that sometimes they weren't.

He gave me his military address so I could send him fishing reports. Sometimes he would send back surplus gear, like the can openers they used to open rations. I put one on my key chain and sliced open several pants pockets before I figured out how to keep it folded shut.

Other times, I went weeks without hearing from him. I figured he was busy building bridges and things during those weeks, so I kept the fishing reports going his way in case he needed something to read late at night.

One day, a larger package showed up and inside was a heavy coat, drab olive with a Seabee logo of an angry wasp on the pocket. The material felt like fine canvas, a heavier fabric than pants or shirts were made from. The breast pocket snapped shut and the two side pockets were designed for warmth. The jacket had that indestructible feel of all army surplus wear, and it soon became my go-to jacket anytime there was a chill.

The year I turned eighteen, the Selective Service had eliminated the draft and instead gone to a lottery based on birthdays. I was a college freshman and those of us with birthdays in the lottery chipped in a dollar apiece for a kitty to go to the guy with the lowest number. Due to a mistake at the student union, by my name on the board someone wrote the number eight. That made me the lowest man on the totem pole and a sure bet to be called up. It took less than thirty seconds for me to decide I would enlist in the Navy as a Seabee.

Someone caught the error soon afterward and my number was changed to 208. Dad and I had talked about the service on a late-night fishing trip the summer before. He had paid a price, he said, that he thought might cover at least my generation. He'd been hit shortly after the Battle of the Bulge. He had a tough time of it, going through field hospitals and then on to a hospital in London. He made it out more from gumption than anything else.

He said that it was my decision, though he did have a preference. He said he wanted his kids to be the first in the family to finish college. So I stayed in school. And all three of us kids finished college.

During those college years, my Seabee jacket went where I did. When I joined the Forestry Club, the patch went on my Seabee jacket. I wore it to bonfires, on hunting trips, and on winter hikes to chase brook trout in the mountains. When I got home, it went with me on night fishing trips and winter trolling expeditions.

Over the years, that coat sheltered me against the cold north winds in the mountains of Virginia and through snowstorms in the Rockies. Rolled up, it served as a pillow when I camped. The Seabee logo faded some, the sleeve cuffs frayed, but the coat survived.

Sometimes, I notice it hanging in the back of a closet when I reach for another jacket. It seems like the one anchor through turbulent decades that saw streakers, hippies, protests, and presidential assassinations.

Whenever I flip back through old photo albums and find a fishing snapshot with a line of fish ready to be cleaned, I can't help but notice my shaggy hair poking out from under a college stocking cap and the jacket that is always there. Perhaps that coat was meant to protect me from chill winds, but I often think it protected me from more than that. Since JC wasn't there to look after me himself, maybe this was his way of defending me from all that was going on around me.

JC did make it home from Vietnam. He taught his Seabee skills to youngsters in high school shop class, things like welding and machine skills. He retired not long ago and now lives on a lake where he still wins the local bass tournaments. I always knew he had a sixth sense for fish ever since he found that crappie bed.

The Seabee jacket still hangs in the closet with my fishing clothes. The miles and memories took their toll. Stains spot the elbows and loose threads hang off the seams. It looks a little worse for wear, much like the kid with the shaggy hair who first put it on fifty years ago.

I need to find JC so we can go fishing again. Maybe I'll take along the jacket and share all the memories, each one with its own stain. The stories would fill the time between fish and take us back to a lake on a crappie bed years ago.

Maybe those stories would help fulfill a debt I still owe JC, not for the Seabee jacket, but for what it stood for. We all own some of that debt. I'm just the one with the jacket that reminds me.

After Dark

After darkness pulls the shades down, movement begins on the other side. Imagination pokes us in the ribs, and some of what we fear begins to walk the earth. Those who venture out after dark know what I mean.

Years ago, Dad and I spent most Saturday nights on the lake with a Coleman lantern hanging over the side of our boat. While it hummed, we would settle into a soft state of listening to night noises and anything over that drone seemed jarring.

On the occasion of a rod dipping, we'd lean over the side to see the surprise come to the surface. Sometimes a small catfish, other times a crappie. One night, we had a force of shad minnows running laps around our lantern when Dad's rod bounced. He lifted it and started to swing on board a crappie so thin that the lantern light shone through. A flared mouth and gills followed it into the light and scared Dad so badly he yanked the crappie right out of a trophy largemouth's grasp. Such is the state of nerves on a quiet night.

On another evening, we were backed up to a cliff on the remote end of the lake. The cliff leaned in toward the lake as it went up, sheltering us and reflecting our lantern light. Just after dark, as the world grew quiet, we heard a wildcat scream in the distance. Dad started telling stories.

Most of them were old folktales of men who mistook the wildcat's scream for a woman in distress and followed her through the mountains never to be seen again. Other stories related to farm animals disappearing without a sound and only tracks left behind.

Those who fish all night know that there is a time when a lull sets in, as if the creatures pause to catch their breath. The sounds soften, the lantern dims, and lines lay slack. On a normal night, it's a signal to pump the lantern and put on fresh bait. Maybe freshen up the coffee.

But on this night, just as our eyelids seemed their heaviest, from atop the cliff over our heads, as if signaling his mad dive into our boat, the wildcat screamed. That piercing vocalization chilled us and sent shivers as surely as opening the door to a meat locker. I felt like a cartoon character that mentally leapt, leaving his clothes in the air on the way up and threading back into them on the way down.

Maybe the cat had followed the light or just claimed the cliff as the edge of his territory. Either way, it didn't matter.

We left.

Sometimes, it's the people you fish with who make the night more interesting. I had a jumpy uncle named Wally who liked to fish, but night was not his favorite time to be out. You could see his nervousness as he fidgeted and constantly looked behind him.

We took Wally trout fishing after dark. In the summer, the trout congregated in the deep parts of the lake where they could descend until they found cold water. We'd anchor where a hundred feet of rope might be exhausted to reach bottom or let the boat drift until the anchor touched and held.

This trip took place back in the sixties, when reports of UFOs dominated the tabloids. About an hour into the trip, we had a trout or two in the cooler, the chatter in the boat was upbeat, and it was shaping up to be a fine night. Suddenly, a flash went across the sky like an exploding plane crashing down. It appeared so close that it seemed to fall just over the ridge across the lake. Wally was the first to comment.

"What was that?"

Obviously, none of us knew, but Dad was never one to miss an opportunity for a prank.

"You know, they've been seeing those UFOs all over the place."

"Seeing what?"

"Yeah, those spaceships. People say they've been coming down to check us out. Some say they take people back with them."

"Say what?"

"Sure, I heard one fellow say they killed one of his cows. Only took parts of it and left the rest in the field."

"You think they landed over there?"

By now, Wally's knees were bouncing, and he was looking around as if they might be sneaking up behind us. The way our light ended just out of casting range, they could get close before we saw them.

We found out the next day that a giant meteor had hit the ground in Ohio but created such a flare that it was visible in ten states. Where we sat, it seemed right next door.

None of this, however, did Wally any good. By now, he was sure he'd seen an alien spaceship. And Dad just kept needling him, obviously having more sport with Wally than with the trout.

"You don't think they'd come out here, do you?"

"They could if they wanted to," replied Dad. "I'm sure if they can fly through space they can fly over here."

Wrong answer. Wally slid into a visible state of agitation a boat could hardly contain. His knees were bouncing, and his head rotated like an owl's, watching for aliens on all sides. Finally, he said what he was obviously thinking.

"I want to go home."

We left.

After dark, some boats are just too small for our imaginations.

Fishing Directions

Farm ponds often provide outstanding areas for fishing since they are remote and fished less than public waters. So when an invitation to fish a private pond came my way, I pounced on it. Three friends who overheard the conversation followed suit.

The pond reportedly had bass and bluegill populations so thick that fishermen lined up to bring their kids here fishing. Therefore, four experienced fishermen should have no trouble at all, or so we thought.

"You probably won't be able to find it," said our host on the phone. "I'll have my husband meet you at the Dairy Queen at eight tomorrow morning."

Later that night, I located the Dairy Queen address and calculated the travel time to be a few minutes early. The spare time quickly dissolved the next morning as we gathered gear, found breakfast, and needled each other as fishermen tend to do. Visions of largemouth danced in our heads.

We pulled into the Dairy Queen parking lot five minutes early. Being the only vehicle in the lot, it was evident our host had not arrived. We're not too sharp at eight in the morning but we figured out this much.

A cat with a passel of kittens roamed just outside the dog exercise fence, apparently there to taunt them. Or maybe the cats were there to make the dogs run around frantically so they tired more quickly, and travelers could put them back in their cars and be on their way sooner. Some people think of everything.

About 8:15, no one had shown up yet, so we surmised they were late. Remember my earlier comments on our powers of deduction.

I called our host and she apologized profusely, recommending that it might move us along more quickly if we met someone else who knew the pond's location. They were supposed to be at her cabin and she gave us directions to get there. The pond, we were assured, was close by.

About twenty minutes later, we pulled into the driveway by the cabin and noticed someone outside. Figuring that must be our contact, I walked over and introduced myself. As our luck or lack of it would indicate, this wasn't who we were supposed to meet.

It was, however, another fisherman who had gone to the public lake nearby and had an outstanding day crappie fishing. Unable to pull away without insulting someone who might be able to point me to my contact, I politely listened to his fishing report on a banner crappie trip.

After what seemed a long time, I cut in and asked if he could tell me where to find the fellow I was looking for.

"Oh, he's not here," replied the fisherman and went straight back to his fishing story.

I got back on the phone with my host, and she again apologized profusely.

"I'm almost there," she added. "Just get in your truck and drive back the way you came. We'll meet on the road."

So we again loaded into the truck and started driving back the way we had come.

It seemed we had driven too far so we pulled off into a church parking lot to wait for our host to pass by. At this point, my passengers were making snide remarks and I began to think it might be easier to manage those feral cats back at the Dairy Queen.

Our host didn't drive by during the next few minutes, so I called again. As it turned out, she had also pulled over to wait for us to drive by her. While we talked, I looked down the road and saw her wave.

Now able to follow her, we made it down a dirt road to one of the fishiest ponds I've ever seen. A broad, shallow body of water, it was splotched with brush, small islands, and a few standing trees.

We listened as our host provided a background on when the pond was built and stocked, as well as a few pointers on where we might bump into a snake or two.

We all shuffled our feet and discretely checked our watches while trying to be polite and attentive, antsy to finally fish. After what seemed like eternity but was in fact five minutes, she left us to our fishing.

We quickly split up and headed to what looked to each of us as the fishiest water. The shadows receded from the corners and soon the bright sunlight fell on the entire pond. I looked at my watch and guessed our trip had taken two hours of the best fishing time.

With each of us taking a different side of the pond, we quickly covered the water and converged back at the truck to compare notes.

I had thrown popping bugs on a fly rod, another had tossed artificial worms, while the other two had cast hard baits. We had driven two hours in all directions, cast and covered water in a pond that regularly produced for young fishermen, and luckily managed to avoid the snakes.

For all our efforts, we had not one bite.

At this point, we decided to eat lunch. That is, if we could still find the Dairy Queen.

Old Guys
in a Boat

Old guys bring more than tackle with them into the boat.

The striper bite was slow. The rods bobbed with the gently rocking boat as it drifted over the old river channel in the upper end of the lake. Twenty feet below, herring minnows swam in varying degrees of shimmies as fish passed but didn't eat. One of the guys poured a cup of coffee and rested it on his knee while he screwed the cap back on the thermos and then slowly sipped.

"You remember that time . . ." his buddy began, the way tellers of old stories always do. It's a rhetorical question because buddies always remember. Then the dam breaks and stories flow like a flash flood:

". . . we tied a plastic fish on your dad's line when he wasn't looking?"

A smile crosses the other fisherman's face.

"Sure, but he deserved it. He was always pulling something on someone. Once he had two guys that wanted him to take them squirrel hunting on the lake, so he let one out on a point that was part of a small island. Then he drove around until he confused the other one and let him out on the other end of the island. They didn't have two hundred yards of timber between them."

"Why did he do that?"

"Probably so they wouldn't ask him again. Besides, they would be easy to find when he picked them up at dark."

"Wasn't it your idea to tie the plastic fish on his line?"

"Yeah, we owed him one. So we waited that night until it got late and we caught one of his lines, pulled it up, and tied the fish on. Then before letting it go, we gave a tug to look like a bite and he pulled the fish in."

"Remember those guys in the other boat seeing that red plastic fish in the lantern light and wanting to know what kind it was? Your dad was laughing so hard he could hardly talk. Then he told them it was a rainbow. That was when we started laughing."

"He was a character. He'd make you pay if you fell asleep night fishing with him. He'd watch until your head started bobbing, and then he'd yell at the top of his lungs, 'Hit it!' When you asked him what that was all about, he'd smirk and say he thought the fish needed some encouragement."

"Remember when your dad closed his taxidermy shop and had all those leftover animals in the basement? We had a lot of fun with them."

"I must have gotten the prankster genes from his side of the family. What was it you called that hunting buddy of yours that always stretched the truth?"

"Houji."

"Remember the time we set up camp with Houji to deer hunt?"

"And you brought the stuffed pheasant?"

"Yeah, and before daybreak you got Houji to help you gather firewood and led him to the pheasant?"

"I told him it was a grouse that was asleep and he should club it with one of the sticks so we could eat it for dinner."

"Then when he did, all that stuffing blew up and the head sprung out like a jack-in-the-box. Houji stood dumbfounded for about thirty seconds before he squawked, 'It's stuffed!'"

"Well, it did keep him from lying so much that trip."

"Just until lunch. As I recall, he saw more deer that afternoon than the rest of us combined, or so he said. Of course, he didn't shoot any, so he probably made it up."

The guys grinned and each checked his bait to make sure it still had some wiggle. The boat traffic was light, and they had seen no gull activity. The sun rose in the bluebird sky, making them drowsy with the warmth.

"You know, it's a wonder we didn't flunk out of college."

"It wasn't the fishing so much as the random things. Sometimes you pay for your mistakes later than you expect, but you usually pay."

"Tell me about it."

One of the lines started angling off toward the front of the boat. The two fishermen watched until they knew the fish was committed, and then the angler in the front picked up the rod and set the hook. Then the fish made a run.

"What do you think it is?"

"Feels like a small striper. Just not enough pull to be too heavy."

As the fish approached the boat, it made a couple circles and came close to tangling the other lines before rolling over on its side into the net. About eighteen inches, the striper was quickly released and swam away with a splash of its tail.

"At least we got the skunk off."

"True, but we might still be eating Beanie Weenies for supper."

"Not me. I've got crappie fillets in the freezer."

"I've got some channel cats. You know, we used to put a hurtin' on the channel cats growing up."

"You remember that river we fished on Saturday nights after work?"

"The one that ran into Smith Mountain Lake? Sure, we never came away empty from a night there. Seemed like there was always one in that hole at the bend that wanted to test our tackle."

"We'd get home so late it was hard to roll out for church."

"Well, you slept through it anyway."

"Or got bruised ribs from Mom's elbow."

"Then if someone offered us a spot in a boat that afternoon, off we'd go again."

"Maybe youth isn't always wasted on the young."

"We're not old, just high mileage."

"Maybe you, but I'm old."

"Well, you're still fishing."

"True enough."

The flow of words slowed to a trickle after that. The fishermen began pulling in their lines without a word announcing that the trip was over. They had fished together long enough to recognize the end without having to discuss it.

Their used bait was tossed for passing gulls. Their rods were stowed in the same places for the umpteenth time and any loose tackle was tucked into cubby holes where it belonged.

Words may serve to pass the time in a boat, but there also comes a point when time needs to be slowed just for a little. That's especially true when two old guys come together in a boat and bring more than just tackle. They also bring a mutual history that comes alive with the telling of it. And, for a morning, the guys can choose which parts they live again.

A Lesson
Twice Learned

Teenage boys compete. Take any sport and the best of friends; they will bounce off each other until the pecking order is established.

Rick and I knew our pecking order; I was his wingman. On the basketball court, he racked up points while I racked up assists. On the baseball team, we both played second base, but I played it from the bench. The one pursuit where I held my own was on a trout stream with a fly rod.

Opening day on a mountain trout stream can empty a town and fill a river. Many locals waded into streams once a year just on this Saturday. Families had picnics, kids hid secret baits in small creels, and the best holes were already staked out. It was a circus without elephants and the blue sky was our big top.

Rick and I arrived early and picked a riffle that fell into a deep pool. To access it, we walked a trail along the edge of a cornfield for a hundred yards after leaving the road. The ground had been turned and the bottomland smelled of wet sand and rotting corn stalks, pungent and rich.

The season opened at noon, and we were standing on the bank by eleven to lay claim to our spot. I wore heavy chest waders with the rubber chipping off from use. When the season was open, I fished. Rick wore hip waders and had already clipped his metal stringer to his belt confident it would soon be filled. The eight hooks jangled against his leg when he walked.

Around the hole, fishermen joked about who had the fastest watch. We agreed that the earliest one was official, and its owner signaled the season's opening by making the first cast. By the time his lure hit the water, every other line was in the air.

On this section of the river, the regulations allowed us to fish with bait, so Rick and I each had a cup of night crawlers in our vest pockets. We still used fly rods, however, in some small concession to the sport of trout fishing.

After the initial flurry, the action paused as if fish and fishermen needed to catch a breath. From upstream, a drifting object caught my eye and I stopped to watch as a fisherman came floating into my view.

He bobbed along in the current feet first and toes high, his waders having trapped air in the feet. His posture resembled that of a fellow reclining in a lawn chair after mowing the lawn on an August afternoon. Holding his rod above water with one hand, he waved with the other as he drifted through the hole, much as he might have had he been pushing off in a yacht on its maiden voyage. He kept his chin barely above water and his sheepish grin offered silent apology.

Apparently, the fisherman had seen all the fish being caught in our pool and was attempting to cross the river upstream to take part from the other side. The current proved too strong, so he became a bit of flotsam floating downstream.

In this opening-day circus, his performance drew only mild interest. He got a few greetings and was asked more than once if he was having any luck. No one complained or threw rocks at him for spoiling our fishing. He was just another clown filling the time between the main acts.

He bobbed around the bend and likely emerged at the next promising hole. The fish seemed momentarily perturbed by the interruption but within minutes began to feed again.

Midday turned into early afternoon and the fish bit in spells. The sun glistened on the surface and reflected from the silver sides of fish as they moved. Each flash drew a cast and either put them down or resulted in a bite.

During the pauses, Rick and I studied each other's stringer to count fish. Whenever one of us pulled ahead, the person who was trailing fished a little harder.

The limit on this stream was eight trout; we both hit seven about the same time. Getting that last fish became a mental challenge, just like taking a final jump shot at the buzzer. Time seemed to tick off and sideways glances checked the other's line as often as our own.

Our eighth fish came simultaneously. We played them delicately to avoid losing the fish, since that would have put one of us in second place. I netted mine and clipped him on my stringer. Then I secured my hook on the rod and sloshed to the bank.

Looking over my shoulder, I noticed Rick had taken one more cast. We both knew he had his limit. Later, he would say he did it on a lark. But looking back, I think the competitor in him wanted to have one more fish.

And he did. A rainbow trout latched onto his night crawler and was soon in hand.

Rick could have released the fish and claimed a moral victory, but instead he slid the trout headfirst down inside his right hip boot. Glancing around the hole, he knew his ninth fish had been noticed so he joined me at the bank to walk back to his car.

The walk through the cornfield was like a postgame celebration without the high fives. We felt we had won and were jubilant. Our steps were brisk and light until we met an older gentleman in drab green blocking the path.

Our local game warden had dedicated much of his career to watching this river. As he neared retirement, gravity had taken its toll; his chest had settled just above his belt to make his shadow square. His grizzled beard was gray and stubbled, always looking like he had last shaved two days ago.

The warden had a cabin downstream and the hole in front of it was named after him. His stern countenance had been honed from years of chasing scofflaws off his river.

"Looks like you boys did all right," he said as he greeted us.

"Yes, sir," we replied in unison. Country boys were brought up with manners, if nothing else, even more so when their elders wore a badge.

"What they bitin'?" he asked.

"I got mine on night crawlers," said Rick.

"Same here," I added.

At this point, all the warden had been doing was chatting. He hadn't asked for our licenses or counted our catch. But he seemed to suspect something was fishy and was stretching the encounter to let it play out. That's when it happened.

The trout in Rick's hip wader started to flap.

When a dying trout begins to give up its ghost, it often makes one last strenuous effort to escape. This one started slapping its tail against the rubber boot with the staccato rhythm of a pileated woodpecker hammering a dead tree. The sound was unmistakable.

I stared straight ahead, and Rick coughed as if the noise would drown out the flopping fish.

Our game warden continued to make small talk. At first, I thought he might not have heard the fish. Surely his hearing wasn't that bad. The slapping fish tail would be recognizable to anyone who had heard the sound before and our game warden must have heard it plenty.

At this point, the warden's voice was like the cicadas' humming, just background noise filling the air. Nothing he said required a response or attentive nod. His words were like the slow ticking of a wall clock during the last period of school while we waited for the bell to ring and set us free.

Rick shifted in place to press his leg against the trout and pin it harder to his wader. The move made the fish start flopping all over again.

By now it was clear we all knew that there was a fish in that boot.

The warden showed no sign of interest in the flapping coming from the wader. He talked on about all the fishermen and what a fine day we had to be out. He mentioned catching a few boys down the river with too many fish, explaining that he had written them tickets that would cost them dearly in court. Possibly hundreds of dollars each.

Looking back, I think he had decided to give us our judgment there on the trail by the cornfield. He let us stew a bit, taking payment from us by letting us simmer in worry and dread while making sure we knew that he knew. At any time, he could have reached for his ticket book and asked Rick for his license. But he didn't.

He grinned and instead said, "Well, I best get on down to the river and check licenses. Anybody on the water this long probably has too many fish."

He gave us a wave and ambled down the path to the river.

Rick and I looked at each other in disbelief and then made a hasty retreat to his car.

We still talk from time to time, now fifty years later, and invariably that fishing trip comes up. Laughing, we argue over who really caught the most fish and talk about an old warden and how his intent was not to exact punishment but to teach us a lesson. Instead of punishing one young man, he chose to instruct two.

He succeeded in that.

Fishing Odd Hatches

The problem with some hatches
is the hatch itself.

Bob White, *Yallerhammer*, pencil on archival paper

Yellow Damn Jackets

You can add any adjective you choose in the yellowjacket's name, and it won't be cussing—it's merely good description.

I have read that as summer progresses yellowjackets become more aggressive. Picnic with watermelon on the spread and you face the prospect of inadvertently munching on these monsters. Fish the backwoods of the Blue Ridge Mountains and you face the prospect of them munching on you.

Early in the morning, the air may cool sufficiently to make these underground wasps sluggish, but the afternoon sun turns a nest into a landmine should you stand on one as I did on such an afternoon.

My attention was turned toward a placid pool about four to five feet deep in the center and confined between two steep banks. Standing high above the water, I had a good observation post to spot fish. Watching for movement, rises, or sides flashing below, I paid my feet no attention until the first pinprick on my arm. Then my attention shifted abruptly.

My sleeve held a few stragglers looking for bare skin, but my waders were barely visible from the knee down. Only then did I notice the menacing hum and quivering wings of yellowjackets so thick they looked like fur. The colony marched north and drastic measures were clearly required. I took three long strides and jumped from the bank as sprightly as a spooked bullfrog.

Hitting the water without concern of its depth or bottom structure, I soon found myself chest deep with the undrowned remnant of the colony buzzing ominously overhead. I discovered that if I kept within six inches of the surface they would come no closer.

I held the front of my chest waders as high as possible to minimize the water intake, though filling my waders from the river was the least of my worries. My intestinal fortitude was all that prevented my filling them from the inside.

I took some consolation that even though I had destroyed any opportunity to fish this hole, I had at least provided a couple hundred morsels to trout downstream should they have a taste for fresh terrestrials. Perhaps enough yellowjackets would flow through a pool downstream to trigger a feeding frenzy. I thought about it and concluded the only patterns in my box with any yellow on them were Tellico Nymphs and Yallerhammers. Maybe they would work.

Exiting on a different trail, I surveyed the damage and concluded it no more than a good rinsing and a single sting. I credit such results more to good training than to good fortune.

My earlier training with yellowjackets dated back to college summers working at a Corps of Engineers lake as an assistant ranger. With my hire, they gave me no authority, badge, or weapons of enforcement. In fact, the main part of my job was to refresh the boundary lines around the government property so timber cutters didn't cross over from private land.

Earlier summer hires had kept the easily accessible stretches up-to-date; however, the remote sections had not been cleared in eight years. My partner and I were to cut a line of sight for surveying and to mark the boundary trees. Clearing line of sight required the lead partner to cut all branches in a three-foot-wide strip and then to slash at chest high any tree previously marked on the line. The partner in the back then painted the slash with a bright-orange stripe.

Most days I worked with a full-time Corps employee. He was a woodsman of the sort that had supplemented his income by poaching ginseng or making moonshine much of his life. Little escaped his attention. The two of us traded off jobs in a rhythm that kept us both reasonably fresh on hot days.

One morning, my usual partner didn't show, so they gave me David, a substitute from another crew. To say David lacked woods skills would be like saying Mickey Mouse had big ears.

The section we were working was far up the headwaters of the lake and most easily accessible by boat. Given the slow pace of the jon boat and outboard motor the government trusted us with, the trip took almost an hour each way. Considering that we worked an eight-hour day, we viewed this as a good thing.

Upon our arrival, David took one look at the machete and volunteered to be the lead whacker. I feigned disappointment and we were off.

We had left off the day before halfway up the ridge in a rhododendron thicket that would have deterred a bear. Our path in came to a dead end with the other side apparently at the top of the ridge. David started whacking.

Knowing I'd have no trouble catching up, I took my time opening the new can of orange paint and stirring it with a stick. The peaceful morning air was interrupted only by birdsong and an exuberant machete.

David's youthful energy led him well into the thicket and far past our original dead end to a new one. As I walked in to begin painting trees, I heard before I saw the angry cloud of yellowjackets. David had worked right past them while they were still undisturbed. Now that moment was gone.

I yelled at David to alert him of his impending doom. When he looked back, panic froze him for an instant and then sent him in exactly the wrong direction, back through his trail, the swarm of yellowjackets, and toward me.

David, running through the swarm, immediately gathered stings and hitchhikers that clung to his back. He had already worked up a sweat, having started at a fast pace. When he ran, the T-shirt momentarily left his back and the stings subsided; when he stopped the wet shirt clung to his skin, letting the stingers penetrate.

Seeing disaster running my way, I turned and tried to outpace it. It was nip and tuck as I tried to run with a full bucket of sloshing paint.

David ran in bursts. Every time he thought he had cleared the swarm he would stop and the yellowjackets clinging to the back of his T-shirt stung again, making him think the swarm had caught up. He would yelp, scream adjectives and exclamations, and sprint faster, closing on me and bringing the stinging mayhem with him.

I was struggling to run with the full bucket without splashing it all over me. With David and the yellowjackets gaining, I concluded the government had more orange paint and I threw the bucket up the hill. It struck an oak tree near the trail about waist-high and bottom-first. As every action has an equal and opposite reaction, the paint rebounded in a wide stream just as David passed, effectively painting one side of him orange from ear to ankle.

We ran until we reached the boat. I spun him around and brushed the remaining yellowjackets off his back. I was winded and unscathed; David had a couple dozen stings and was orange.

Our contrast could hardly have been greater. Having merely walked up the hill with a bucket of paint, my workday had yet to begin. David, having been swinging a machete, running from a swarming host of yellowjackets, and taking a dousing of orange paint, appeared to have just survived a wreck involving a Sherwin-Williams truck.

As we sat gasping, David was the first to speak. All he said were four words: "I might be allergic."

We managed the trip back without any episodes, the little outboard running at maximum speed and my angle of travel clipping all the points in a straight line to shorten our path. Back at headquarters, I turned David over for a trip to the doctor and had to explain why I had painted my partner. All I really needed to say was "yellowjackets" and everyone understood.

From that summer on, yellowjackets have been my primary nemesis whether in deep woods or campgrounds. I learned a lot about them in a single summer.

First, do what it takes to get away. This includes jumping in deep water or painting your partner orange. Second, never run toward the guy with the paint bucket. And third, if you get stung and screaming adjectives helps, do it. The little dastards probably deserve a good tongue-lashing.

Carpy Diem

For the sake of full disclosure, I caught my first carp on a fly rod over fifty years ago. Here's how it happened.

Back then, parents thought turning kids loose outdoors amounted to training in independence. So my cousin and I made plans to camp for a week as soon as school was out. He had just gotten his driver's license and I was a couple years younger and happy to have a ride. We headed to a public campground at the lake.

I had an Eagle Claw fiberglass fly rod that I used back then to fish the bluegill beds. I also took along some spin-fishing gear for bass. Our plan was to walk the banks and fish for our supper.

As it turned out, a Boy Scout troop also set up in the campground to train for a canoe race. They each had a canoe and planned to paddle for strength training. Their plan was to spend each day on the lake paddling for miles. Having some deadweight in the bow was a plus for their training, even if that deadweight was casting a fly rod.

Soon after pushing off from the bank, we noticed the surface of the lake was riddled with the wakes of fish as if small sharks cruised the waters. Whenever the fish came upon something floating, a round orange mouth broke the surface and slurped it in. These objects looked from a distance like black wine corks. Up close, they could easily be recognized as locusts.

Their "pharaoh" droning hovered over the lake like Muzak. I convinced my Boy Scout paddler to push into some overhanging branches which I shook and littered the canoe floor with bugs. I rigged one and prepared to sight fish for carp.

On our first attempt, we slid delicately into the path of a cruising carp. Carefully I took aim and lofted my buzzing bug in its path. Then I waited.

The locust sent out vibrations more appealing than a chummed blood trail to a shark. You could see the carp turn toward the vibration, line up, and slurp without pausing. Upon the hookset, the carp took off and we were in pursuit.

The locusts that the carp preferred still had life in them and vibrations emanated out like distress signals when they hit the water. These same insects had minds of their own on the cast, sometimes deciding to fly in an unintended direction.

For instance, your backcast might come buzzing by the back of your head sounding like a swarm of angry bees or the locust could defy participating in anything that resembled a loop. Everything it contacted, the locust grabbed, whether line, leader, or limb.

Finding a cruising carp willing to eat wasn't the challenge; the problem was casting a large insect that might decide to fly midcast. You could pinpoint your aim, only to have your fly take off like it caught an ill wind. But anytime I placed the locust in front of a carp and the fish sensed the wing vibrations emanating across the water, the fish homed in on the bug and we were on.

The carp were mostly four-pounders with a few a tad heavier. The bigger ones could drag the canoe in a sleigh ride that gave my paddler a rest. With plentiful bait, a willing paddler, and no shortage of fish, it soon became too much of a good thing.

We tried locusts along the bank, hoping for something we could eat for dinner. At one submerged beech tree I lofted a locust directly over it. Slowly, a largemouth rose and opened its mouth in a way that got him its name. I could see the red gills and braced for the bite so I wouldn't jerk the bug out of its mouth. Just as it reached the surface, it seemed to spot our canoe and turned brashly, slapping the bug with its tail.

A few bluegill tried to munch on the locusts, usually chipping away at the underbelly and not taking the entire bug. Still, they attacked each one I put in their vicinity and would peck away if it was left in their reach.

Late that evening, we went back out with spinning gear to plug topwater for bass. I caught five carp on a black Hula Popper. I kept changing lures trying to find one that carp wouldn't eat and bass would, but I never found the key to that dilemma. Though we had planned to fry our fish, we preferred Spam and Vienna sausages to any carp recipe.

So for the rest of the week, we amused ourselves with carp on locusts. By the time we broke camp, my fly casting with a moving bait had improved but it left me with having my fill of carp.

Now when I read the stories of fly fishing for carp, I have to wonder if someone is not masterminding a colossal joke on the fly-fishing world. You can see the clues if you look for them.

For instance, someone seems to be orchestrating an ingenious marketing campaign. Take the nickname they came up with—freshwater bonefish. Here they've stolen a fish's reputation, namely, one that people spend thousands of dollars to pursue in remote places and attached that halo to a carp.

A carp is to a bonefish as a VW Beetle is to a Maserati. Bonefish are sleek speed machines, and the dealership is located on an ocean island. Carp are stubby workhorses with good mileage, a rusty color, and can be found in seedy neighborhoods.

Fishermen often remark that trout don't live in ugly places. Well, carp do. They inhabit waters that the Environmental Protection Agency has on their watch list. Instead of majestic mountains in the background, you are more likely to fish for carp in the shadows of an apartment building.

And most grip-and-grin shots are more likely to make others grin at your carp than be jealous. Replace that carp with an equal-sized salmonid and Facebook will light up with requests for directions to your beat. Carp photos bring jeers and jokes.

Partly it's because carp are just plain ugly. These fish must be unattractive to each other as well since they normally spawn in muddy water. If you want to scare a roommate, just tape a headshot of a carp to his bathroom mirror first thing in the morning. His scream can serve as your alarm.

Even hooking these fish is interesting. For instance, you can't hook a carp in the corner of the mouth. Circles don't have corners. So your fly design needs to compensate for being sucked through an opening the size of a grape.

Once you hook a carp, the fight is sort of methodical, to be polite. Sure, the first run can take some line and the fish has certainly mastered zigzagging. But I've never had a carp go airborne.

I should add that I have never taken an Asian carp on a fly. Seeing the videos of all these fish jumping simultaneously does make me wonder if I'd just get confused on which one I was fighting.

Having said all this, I will confess to fly fishing for carp on occasion. Primarily, I wait seventeen years between seasons to catch that one special hatch. To be on a slick lake sight casting to cruising carp is indeed a special way to fish. Large black flies fished with minor vibrations are deadly.

In between these hatches, I struggle to convince myself to go chasing carp. In the back of my mind, I imagine some old, white-haired advertising executive standing in pristine waters catching trout after trout, all the while chuckling softly to himself.

The reason he's chuckling in my mind's eye is that he's the one who came up with the campaign to promote carp fishing. And he did it to lighten the pressure on his favorite trout stream.

If I can ever meet him, I'd like to go fishing with this guy at least for a day. Even if it's just for carp during a locust hatch, sort of a carpy diem.

Along Came
a Spider

You never know what is going to happen on a trout stream. The fish of a lifetime may emerge from the shadows and inhale your streamer. An otter may glide through the hole and come up with a trout that was a fraction too slow. Or a heron may challenge you for fishing rights on your favorite pool. What you don't expect, or welcome, is to hear a bloodcurdling scream.

The morning started like many trips in the late fall. A light frost covered the low spots and the exposed bank had ice crystals where the water lapped up during the night. The leaves had mostly blown down, the few remaining crackling in the trees with the slightest breeze, brown and past their vibrant fall colors.

The stream now held most of the leaves, or so it seemed. With each fall rain, they would relocate driven by high water, swept into slower pools, or piling up on the inside bends where the current couldn't carry them farther. When the leaves hid rocks, you could easily stumble through the unseen and uneven bottom, tweaking an ankle, and splashing far more than you wanted.

My daughter and I had chosen to fish a mountain tailrace, partly because we knew the water level would be good and partly because the fishing would be predictable. Every fall and winter, you could drift nymphs or eggs and have a good day. Watching repeated drifts through pockets and gullies for the slightest tick lets a person relax and get excited at the same time.

My daughter has also fished long enough to learn most of what I know, so the main reason I keep an eye on her is to enjoy watching her catch fish. Though we never get too competitive, the outcome can influence the dialogue on the ride home. Bragging rights come with the right to brag.

So that is how we fished this morning. She was upstream fishing alone where a riffle dumped into a large pool. I was downstream but in sight, drifting a stonefly nymph between rocks to pick up stragglers in the broken water.

We had each picked up a few fish early. The sun had risen over the ridge just minutes earlier and began to lift the chill. Small swirls of fog rose where the frost evaporated from exposed rocks. Somewhere downstream, wood smoke from a cabin drifted through the gorge and just the smell of it warmed us.

The scene looked like something that Norman Rockwell might have painted for Thanksgiving with father and daughter spending a day on the river. The woodsmoke contributed to the mood and the sun warmed us in contrast with the chilling water lapping against our waders. If I could have described the mood in one word, it would have been "tranquil."

That's when I heard the scream.

Maybe "scream" is too strong a word. Something between a loud gasp and the noise you make just before you go into shock. The sound was definitely loud enough to shatter any mood of tranquility, like a Christmas ornament dropping on a slate floor. Looking upriver, I saw my daughter standing on the edge of the pool holding her line dangling in front of her with what looked from the distance like a tiny leaf on her egg pattern.

I scurried to the bank, curious and a little anxious, and hustled up to where she fished. When I waded out to her and asked what was wrong, she looked at me with amazement and replied, "I caught a spider."

What appeared to be a tiny leaf from downstream turned out to be a brown spider, wrapped up around the egg like a second layer. Balled up, it would have fit on a dime.

The spider's legs hinged perfectly around the egg to form a cage as if it expected the egg to escape. It had probably developed this habit for grabbing insects that did attempt to get away.

Besides being wet and tenacious, the spider looked like any other brown spider that might nest under a porch light to make a living off the insects the light attracts. Its legs had tiny hairs that made it all the creepier. In short, it just looked like a spider except it wasn't supposed to be on the end of a fly line.

"Did you catch him on your backcast?" I asked, trying to figure out how you would catch a spider.

"No, I didn't get my line near the woods," she said. "He came out of that pile of leaves right there."

She pointed to a slow spot on the inside of the riffle where leaves piled up as thick and broad as a mattress. The water above the leaves was at least two feet deep.

As an aside, since that trip I have studied aquatic spiders. Apparently one type will capture an air bubble and go to the bottom to hunt underwater. This one had seemingly been hunting in the leaf pile for small insects. Finding an egg pattern instead, the spider had latched on and now defended its lunch.

Looking at the spider, I asked if she had tried to take him off. She responded with a stare from her teenage years that translated to, "You must be out of your mind."

So we swapped rods and I slapped her egg against the water. The spider held on. I tried again, harder, and it still hung on.

We looked at each other with a mix of thoughts. One, this was one tough spider. Two, the river we waded in through many seasons of warm and cold weather had spiders that lived underwater. They lived around our feet, but we had never seen them. We knew to avoid copperheads after the spring weather arrived and yellowjackets in the late summer and the early fall, when they are most aggressive. Now we also had in our minds that spiders crept on the bottom in still water.

Which still left us with a spider clinging to the egg pattern.

"You know, a fish might eat him," I offered jokingly.

She gave me another look that translated to, "Feel free to fish with him yourself."

To get my rod back, I returned to slapping the spider and egg heartily against the water. After it finally conceded, we switched rods.

I said, "That was quite a spider. He really wanted to eat your egg."

To which she replied, "I don't think so. He was too intense. I think he was trying to mate with it."

From time to time, I tie up a few extra flies for my daughter to restock her fly box, usually patterns I use most often so if I start catching fish, she has a duplicate. It seemed appropriate that the next batch I gave her included egg patterns with spiders already on them.

She accepted the gift with another look I knew. The memory of her earlier experience with the spider would keep these out of her fly box for the simple reason that they might work like decoys and attract a real one. Or if a real spider slipped in to grab an egg once again, she might not recognize it thinking it was one of my impostors.

I no longer worry about spiders living underwater around my feet. Nor do I lose much sleep over yellowjackets or snakes. They just go with the territory. One thing does cause me to tread lightly at times, like a kid crossing a graveyard at night when he believes in ghosts. I wait with anticipation, look over my shoulder, and expect the worst.

I don't know when it will happen, but I know it will. That one thing I worry about is how my daughter will get even for giving her egg patterns with spiders on them.

Paybacks can be hell.

Fishing the Mosquito Hatch

My fishing library is littered with manuals on the insects that trout eat, including stoneflies, caddisflies, and terrestrials. Most of the terrestrial patterns are for grasshoppers, crickets, beetles, and the occasional caterpillar. Not one book have I found for fishing the mosquito hatch. Probably this is because most of us would rather not.

Still, you can hardly ignore this hatch. There are over 2,500 known species of mosquitoes. The main downside to this is the number of fly boxes you have to carry to match them all.

So just in case you find yourself interested in the mosquito hatch allow me to explain a bit about them. For starters, mosquitoes have a life span of five to six months. This may not seem long to the mosquito, but it can seem like an eternity to you, especially if you forgot your Deet.

During mating season, the males locate their female counterparts by listening for their incessant whining. Although this brings many thoughts to mind, foremost among them is my desire not to become an endangered species. So let me add that no matter the reason behind the female's whining, I am sure it was the male's fault.

For all their motion, mosquitoes move rather slowly. Even by flapping their wings 250 to 300 times per second, they only reach speeds up to three miles per hour.

You should also be aware that swatting them only makes things worse. In doing so, you generate lactic acid and carbon dioxide, which they like, and the motion activates their visual sensors. So the best approach is simply to fish at four miles per hour and outrun the little suckers.

I tried this a few years back near Grand Rapids, Michigan, when I was traveling for business with another fly-fisherman. We decided to fill a gap in our schedule with a side trip to a nearby stream.

Ron, my fishing partner, opted to fish upstream and was soon out of sight. I walked downstream to fish back and quickly found myself on a section that ran through bogs on both sides. The flow slowed and trout actively sipped flies on the surface. I slapped my neck to flatten the first of the hatch to find me.

Casting and swatting simultaneously will quickly convince you that fly fishing is a three-handed sport. I threw in extra false casts hoping to knock a few of these whiners out of the air. The motion caused them to converge, and I steadily lost the battle.

The thicker the mosquito hatch became, the more active the trout were. Clearly mosquitoes were their main course as I was the mosquitoes'. The bogs apparently were prime breeding grounds; based on the number of mosquitoes, I wondered if their evenings involved candlelight and soft music. Perhaps even a little whine.

From my observations, the place could have supported a lot more frogs and bats. I made a mental note to contribute to Frogs Unlimited or form a chapter if none existed.

At some point soon after, I had enjoyed all I could stand so I made a hasty retreat to the bridge where we had parked. The light breeze and the elevation of the bridge made it the one spot out of reach for the mosquitoes.

Ron met me back on the bridge before our agreed time to quit. He looked at me with surprise before asking, "Why aren't you fishing?"

"Mosquitoes," I replied. "Millions and millions of mosquitoes. I hardly fished this section at all."

"Mind if I try?" he asked.

"Be my guest."

I watched Ron wade in below the bridge where I had quit. As he pulled line from his reel, I saw him take the first swat, then the second. He made a cast and began flailing about his head. He tried bringing his arms up near his face to fish with his wrists above his head while protecting his cheeks with his forearms. None of his defenses worked and soon he was on the bridge beside me.

"See what you mean," he offered stoically. Perhaps fishing on his home waters made Hemingway the writer that he was: too many words would cause a fellow to swallow a few mosquitoes.

My general observation on mosquitoes is that the further north you travel the bigger they get, although I have heard that Louisiana claims the mosquito as its state bird. Still, some of the tiniest mosquitoes I've encountered have been in the Southern states.

Once I vacationed on Kiawah Island, South Carolina, at a golf resort. Having given up golf early in life, frankly just moments after my first round, I decided to try fishing the tidal creeks around the island. Trout, flounder, and redfish frequented these waters, and I was up for a tussle with any fish that flipped, wriggled, or cavorted.

Mosquitoes had been no problem at the resort but I found out later they sprayed the place so people could golf and restrict their worries to the alligators in the water hazards. Apparently, gators were the lesser of the two evils.

I reached a tidal creek on the incoming tide with some optimism. The creek was large enough for good fish but tight enough for me to cast across. I began chunking Clousers—one of my favorite fly patterns for exploring new waters—and stripping them through the creek channel.

That's when the no-see-ums saw me.

The problem with a mosquito too small to see is that you can only swat it after it bites. Beforehand, you don't know it's there unless you have a dog's hearing range and can pick up their whine.

The other learning on mosquitoes is that the smaller the bug, the sharper the teeth. Soon after the no-see-ums found me, this outing ended much like the Michigan outing, with a quick retreat to safety.

These two trips taught me a lot about mosquitoes and the need for better gear. I now keep a mosquito net in my fly gear to pull over my head and fish in long-sleeved shirts through the summer. I heavily douse the sleeves and my cap with Deet when fishing a mosquito hatch. Also, I have a Thermacell that occasionally fits the situation, though I fully expect these carnivorous insects to evolve and make the Thermacell scent a homing beacon rather than a repellant.

Where mosquitoes abound, it makes sense that fish eat them regularly. Many of us carry mosquito patterns in our boxes and these are usually sparse tiny flies with grizzly-gray hackles, which do a good job of imitating the blur of wings moving at 250 to 300 beats per second. Apparently, trout can't see them any better than we can. Trout do, however, have an advantage by living under water.

Still, given the numbers of mosquitoes and their life span, it's worth having some of these flies in your box. But when the hatch you are matching is a mosquito, that is a mixed blessing, for what the fish are eating is also eating you.

A Whiff
of Skunk

Sometimes the difference between
getting skunked or not is one bite.

Bob White, *Light Reflected,* pencil on archival paper

Stir Crazy

Winter comes even to the South, especially when you live in the Blue Ridge Mountains. The moods it brings have their own seasons. Initially, the first crisp frost is met with celebration, lighting the fireplace, and anticipating the first snow. Then the hard cold comes, and winter becomes a chore. Toward the end, more time is spent indoors, and the walls begin to inch closer together.

A fisherman's mood in late winter resembles that of the buzzards on an old poster, staring across an empty desert. One turns to the other and says, "Patience hell, I'm going to kill something." Substitute "catch" for "kill" and you have the reason for a late-winter fishing trip when there is no other good reason to go.

Pulling off the road beside Humility Creek, I questioned my own sanity, realized that was what I was trying to salvage, and stepped out to a brisk slap of cold air. Patches of snow lay wherever the shade protected it. The creek had a soft gurgle as much of the free water that fed it was frozen.

Humility Creek is popular and easily accessible, which is its greatest fault. Today, though, I had the stream to myself as fools don't always attract company.

I figured all the trout would be hunkered in deep water and moving as little as possible. My plan then was to dredge the bottom with weighted nymphs, hoping one might wash into the mouth of a trout when it yawned. They were likely too cold to be feeding.

The first hole I came to still lay in the shade as the sun had not topped the ridge behind it. Ice fringed the banks in sheets where the current was slow. Icicles hung off the opposing rock like fangs. Before my fingers could immobilize from the cold, I tied on a weighted stonefly nymph and began to fish.

Perhaps I should say I began to cast. I couldn't prove through my efforts that fish existed here. I saw none and felt none. My nymph bumped the bottom, tapping rocks and coming up with an occasional twig. Once

I caught a caddis casing on the point of the hook, so I knew I was deep enough.

When it's this cold and still, sounds magnify. Trees groan with movement. The only bird calls came from crows, scavenging even today. I was mesmerized by the gurgle of the stream as I cast, followed the nymph with my rod, and cast again.

Like most fishermen, after some time without a bite I began to change flies. First, I went smaller, tying on nymphs I could barely hold even with bare fingertips in a pair of gloves that ended at the middle knuckle. Someday I will find the outlet where they sell all those fingertips and stock up. I don't remember ever having cold palms.

After an hour or so with no bite, I decided to try big flies. Bill's Provider is a local pattern with a promising name, so I tied one on. I reasoned that a fish might move for a mouthful, but my flawed reasoning was what brought me here in the first place.

Whenever I got out on the bank to walk to the next hole, my toes complained about the return of circulation. They went through stages of burning from the first movement to the chill of reality. By the time I reached the next hole, they lobbied not to be submerged again.

Prior to stepping in, I pulled some peppered jerky from my pocket and tore off a chunk. I stuck it into my cheek the way a tobacco user might a wad of Red Man and let the seasoning provide some heat.

By the time I had waded in again, the sun had cleared the ridge and begun to shine coldly on the water. The light felt pale and without energy though I knew it must warm things a degree or two. Still, nothing moved but me and the crows.

I waded across below the pool to get to the sandy side where I would face the deep water. This hole was one of the deepest on Humility Creek, perhaps eight feet deep today. Another creek entered at the top of the hole and a sycamore leaned over the water. Bill's Provider had yet to provide, so I changed flies again.

Wanting to stay on the bottom, I tied on an egg and added a couple split shot. I had no reason to try this pattern except that I hadn't used it yet and none of the others worked. That's about all the confidence I had in it.

The day had become as pleasant as it would be, and I had settled into enjoying it. The cold receded to the back of my mind and the chill on my face reminded me I was alive.

The split shot bounced on the bottom with a gentle tick on my rod tip and I imagined the egg lifting off occasionally to flutter in the current.

Something stopped the fly and I reflexively set the hook. It tightened with the heft of a log on the end, so I stepped toward it and gave an upward flick to see if the fly would dislodge.

Instead, he began to swim.

The morning's pace had convinced me this would be a fishless day, so switching my mindset over to playing fish was like waking up. The fish swam into the depths of the hole and my first impulse was just to see what I had hooked.

The fish settled into deep water and seemed satisfied to stay down there. I turned his head to get it moving and he reluctantly did so.

I could feel the fish shaking his head to loosen the fly, then he swerved back into the current and swam toward the convergence of the two creeks.

We arm-wrestled slowly with neither of us giving much ground. After a few moments, I felt the fish rising, saw the orange spots, and knew he was a sizable brown trout. I had suspected as much from the earlier headshaking.

The crystal-clear water magnified the size of the trout, yet it was a good fish. I slipped in below it and guided the brown into the net. The egg was back in its mouth, and I quickly removed it and began to revive the fish.

It looked about twenty inches or a tad over. I tend to cheat when guessing the size of my own fish so twenty inches is what I net out after guessing and subtracting a couple inches. I've not seen many much bigger on Humility Creek and this one was the best of the season for me here.

The fish quickly recovered in the cold water and swam away spending as little energy as possible. I dried my fingertips on the sleeves of my jacket, took out another wad of peppered jerky, and stuffed it into my cheek.

That brown would be the only fish of the day, and as best I could tell, the only bite. Nothing else took the egg, but as I told myself on the drive home, if you only catch one fish in a day that wasn't a bad one.

The house seemed a little larger when I got home. The walls had inched back into place, the fire lit with a bit more cheer, and a shot of Blanton's Bourbon provided all the antifreeze my bones required after a day on the creek. Even my toes quit complaining after being moved near the fire.

The end of winter now seemed in sight thanks to one good fish. Perhaps going fishing is a good antidote for going stir crazy.

Low Expectations

Sometimes the best days come when you don't expect too much.

During the winter, a person can easily talk themselves out of fishing. Winter rains can push the river out of its banks. Cold nights make fish sluggish. Northern winds chill the bones and tempt a fisherman to crave the warmth of a fire and alternative entertainment. Days like these tend to be memorable, however, simply because successes magnify themselves.

A recent day did all of this for me. Two inches of rain during the previous forty-eight hours made most streams in the mountains difficult if not impossible. Yet cloud cover only let the water chill a few degrees more and the northern winds probably pushed the ducks only a little farther south. My main reason for going, other than cabin fever, was to test a fly I'd been working on for just such conditions. Designed to sink quickly and bounce on the bottom, it should tread amidst the fish when they hunker down.

I won't say more about this fly for two reasons. First, it has promise. Second, I have few secret flies and need more. Perhaps this pattern will be one of them.

Winter fishing conditions do bless fishermen in one way; they can sleep in, rise slowly, and savor an extra cup of coffee. I did all the above. About midmorning, I donned waders and gear by a stream still falling after the rain and running about a foot above normal.

I didn't go directly to my secret fly as the water I started on didn't demand that much weight. I fished proven patterns in places known to hold fish just to see if they were feeding. After an hour, I had managed one twelve-inch brown on a Foxee Clouser. If the fish were feeding, they were clearly on diets.

Still, on a day like this, the first thought as I released the brown was that I'd not be skunked. Some days you expect a double-digit fish count; on others, you're happy not to be skunked. As you can see, I was fishing with low expectations.

The clouds lingered well after the rain, so the sun wasn't going to help warm things up. I looked up at the clouds for a moment, hoping they might part and a beam of sunshine deliver some ray of hope. None came, so I tied on my secret fly after a bit of pondering.

The hole called for a fly like this. The water rushed in at the top and tumbled into a pocket that obscured the bottom. I dropped my secret fly in where the water rushed and let it go where it pleased.

I dropped it on the inside seam on my third cast, and it quickly found bottom, rolling along as it was designed to do until it stopped. I set the hook and felt it set into something solid that didn't budge. Then, it moved ever so slowly.

I played it gingerly, pleasantly surprised, and watched my line circle through the pool. My rod tip shook each time it threw his head to cut me off or throw my fly. Then it came into sight.

The old brown snarled as it circled. Its lip curled and its body thickened enough to make raising its head difficult. He wasn't wasting energy and was far from spent.

The fish searched for direction, so I gave it one. Not wanting to work it unnecessarily, I looked for a quick path to the net that we might mutually agree upon.

Along the inside of this hole, sand had piled in creating a shallow beach. I guided it in this direction and then stepped between it and the deep water. It moved away from me and soon found itself stranded in shallow water. I netted him and began to shake with the adrenaline rush. Stretched out in the net, the brown did a little shaking himself.

After retrieving my secret fly and reviving the old brown, I guessed him closer to twenty-two inches, well beyond anything I expected to catch. Though it harbors a few, this stream gives up large browns grudgingly. So it was already a banner day, having now a nice fish and a secret fly.

Still, in a few hours I'd only managed two bites. My fly box was getting a workout and in bouncing my rig against the bottom, I had already caught a caddis casing. Usually, this happens when winter nymphing and I read it as a favorable sign that my fly was where it should be.

Fishing on upstream, I came to a pair of long flat holes. The lower one had a bit of depth, but the upper was just a flat run less than waist deep.

Nothing here wanted my secret fly, so I went back to the Foxee Clouser. They didn't want it either.

While going through my fly box, intermittently staring at the water for a suggestion, I got one. One lone Blue-winged Olive floated through the deep water and disappeared in front of me.

Going through all the pockets of my sling, stocked primarily for deep fish, I found one small Parachute Adams that was as close as I was going to get. Probably I had forgotten to take it out. I greased my line and leader, added a couple feet of finer tippet, and tied on the Adams.

In South Louisiana, they have a term that best describes the rest of my day: "lagniappe," something thrown in for good measure.

My big brown on a secret fly had been more than enough. Getting to finish the afternoon on dry flies was above and beyond my anticipation.

Rises were few and far between for one good reason; there weren't enough bugs to go around. So once I found a fish, he bit. The fish were looking up and seeing only occasional morsels in the drift.

Normally, this is a stream of picky fish. Even today they would spook, so I fished stealthily upstream, working the water as gracefully as I could, and when I caught a fish that cavorted about, I'd move farther up and let that section rest. Once at the top of the second hole, I'd go back to the bottom of the lower one and start over. This was my beat until the fish told me to move on.

My Adams finally sank from fish slime and the hackle began to unravel. As happens on day trips sometimes, I didn't have a duplicate. So I switched to an emerger of similar size, but totally different colors, and an odd thing happened. My fish on the Parachute Adams were all decent rainbows, yet my first two fish on the emerger were slightly larger browns.

When the emerger began to fish more like a nymph, I switched to a Renegade just to see how picky they were. The first two fish both came up, put their noses against my fly, and never opened their mouths.

By now the sun had dropped behind a ridge and the north wind spoke of a cold front coming behind it. The Olives had stopped fluttering and the occasional dimples in the surface disappeared with them.

I studied the water, thought about one last hole but changed my mind. I was content. Not that I haven't had better days. But these came when days were supposed to be better. To fish high water in cold weather, catch a picture fish, and then finish the day on dry flies like it was an evening in April gave me a reason to turn up my collar and leave a warm fire. Not to mention that I came home with more confidence in my secret fly.

It's one thing to have low expectations and then have them fulfilled; it's something totally different to have low expectations well exceeded.

That would be lagniappe.

Jinxed

The sun baked the farm pond and the fishermen around it like we were all beef roasts in a recipe calling for long low heat. A breeze taunted us occasionally as if someone was lifting the lid to check on our progress. Any moment now, I expected to be poked with a fork.

Typically, by the early fall, mornings feel crisp and wild places teem with energy and motion. But no bass swirled in the shallows chasing minnows. Birds flew reluctantly, keeping mostly to the shade of the woods. Turtles normally sunning on floating logs hid in the cool mud.

When we gathered midmorning to check our results the count took less time than a sneeze. We were all skunked.

One of our group members remarked that the last time he was on a trip this void of fish, two more of us were also present. He suggested we try to find out which of us was the jinx.

I looked around and knew if anyone had an albatross around his neck it wouldn't be because he caught it. Clearly, the observation was correct, and I knew who it was.

The jinx was me.

Let me provide the reasoning and you will see my point.

A couple years ago, I lined up guides out of Charleston, South Carolina, to chase redfish. The trips were booked well in advance. I don't fly fish in saltwater half as much as I would like so the anticipation grew as the date approached.

The week before the trip, I began to eye the weather. A hurricane lay to the southeast, spinning and picking up intensity from the warm water. The spaghetti map of its projected paths suggested that the weathermen had been replaced by first graders with crayons.

To top it off, another front was flirting on the radar to the northeast. I was staying in Mount Pleasant and the hotel guests were clearing out. Both storms were headed our way.

My guide on the second day called and canceled. The guide for the first day suggested we try early. Maybe we could beat the storm. Apparently, he was an optimist.

The light at daybreak split through broken clouds in shafts as it might through the slats of a dilapidated barn. Our plan was to ease out in kayaks, stake them, and wade the grass. As we paddled, a wall of clouds formed off the coast, dark and ominous, advancing as if slowed by its burdens.

When we reached the grass where we planned to fish, my guide expressed his opinion in one word: "Humph." If that's a word. He followed it with, "Well, we're here, we might as well fish."

His enthusiasm didn't inspire; perhaps he just didn't sell it well.

His mood must have been dampened by the two feet of water above normal tide pushed in by the wind. Redfish could tail in the grass, and we would never see them. I cast blindly at any suspicious swirl.

Small crabs skittered by my feet as I waded, fleeing ahead of the storm. Occasionally, the grasses parted and waved either by current or fish splitting them on their way through. Gusts carried the smell of saltwater ahead of the clouds creeping steadily closer.

I needed some fish pictures and suspected fishing time was soon coming to an end, so I convinced my guide to fish along with me. He compromised by dredging the channel with a lead head jig while I cast flies in shallow water. He finally caught a small red, I shot my photos, and we turned back to watching the clouds.

It's only a slight stretch to say we were watching the onset of The Perfect Storm from kayaks. The lightning came first. We paddled for dry ground and chose a spot with the lowest trees. The thunderstorm complained loudly, and the rain beat down drenching the half of me that had been above water level. We split a pack of crackers while huddled under a low pine.

We told stories of earlier storms to convince ourselves we had been through worse. Since I was twice my guide's age, I had stories marinated in the years that must have sounded like the old tales of walking to school barefoot in the snow uphill both ways. Still, the stories added flavor to the crackers.

At the first break in the lightning, we hightailed it back to the ramp and said our goodbyes. He later remarked to a mutual friend that it was the worst conditions of any trip he had ever guided.

By the time I left, Mount Pleasant had two feet of rain and many of the interstate exits were closed. Instinctively, I glanced at the water standing in parking lots expecting to see tailing reds.

Scientific proof requires repeatable evidence, so allow me to continue.

The next year, I decided to get the smell of skunk off my saltwater fly rod and booked another trip. This time I chose to fish at Charlotte Harbor on the west coast of Florida. As the date approached, I again watched the weather. A tropical storm was building off the coast of Africa. I felt the red dot of its laser scope on my forehead.

When I arrived, I met my guide and asked him how he expected the fishing to be. He summed it up in one word: "Humph."

I understood all too well. Guides must have their own language and "Humph" is the key word.

In this case, we had the opposite problem; we were on the side of the storm pulling water out. The grass flats were high and dry.

We gave up on finding reds in the grass and made our living pulling small fish out of pocket water. The variety of fish in the shallows made each catch like reaching into a grab bag. Nothing huge, but enough bites to break the monotony.

The albatross around my neck fluttered just a little.

By the time we reached the ramp that afternoon, the weather forecast had changed. All the spaghetti noodles mapping the storm had converged and pointed straight at us. I kept it a secret that it was aiming for me.

I headed inland, figuring to draw the storm away from the boats, but it banged on them for a couple days with hundred-mile-per-hour winds. I booked a room in a solid-looking hotel and requested to be above ground level just in case.

Two trips, two hurricanes, and no redfish. Clearly the jinx was me.

I admit this openly knowing that my fishing invitations will go the way of the passenger pigeon and the dodo. If I were I on an ancient ship, I'd likely be tossed over the side and deservedly so. My admission is meant to save the crew.

This is not to say I'm giving up chasing reds with a fly rod. On the contrary, I am setting out to break the jinx.

In the meantime, I am avoiding stepping on sidewalk cracks, crossing myself anytime a black cat passes in front of me, throwing salt over my shoulder routinely, and staying away from ladders altogether.

No bananas are kept on land or water and on Friday the thirteenth I avoid sharp objects and most outdoor activities. I stop short of voodoo as it could make the jinx worse, and I shudder to imagine what worse might look like.

I will continue to chase redfish if for no other reason than to check the temperature of my jinx. But for the time being, when I call up a guide and ask about the fishing, I will know in advance what he'll say.

"Humph."

Into the Backing

Rare sights reward a fisherman who spends time in the Blue Ridge Mountains. On occasion, I've crossed paths with solid-white squirrels. A small population is established in an area I fish. Once, I watched a hellbender creep along the bottom of a pool by my feet munching on the remains of a trout. And perhaps most rare of all, on one late evening I saw the backing on my fly reel.

Seeing your backing pass through the tip of your rod is rare on mountain streams for two reasons. First, you need a pool long enough for all your line to be drawn out. Second, you need a fish large enough to take that much line the length of the pool. On one late evening, I had both.

I was fishing a long hole trapped between two steep ridges. In these mountains, no one calls such a place a canyon. More likely, we would call it a holler. The ridges weren't cliffs, and you could walk up the sides if your legs and wind held out, though you would still want to find a deer trail that ran the contours.

This long hole ran a good length through such a deep dark holler. I'm never more specific than that on the location of a fishing hole for less than the price of a good IPA. Even then I'm likely to lie enough to keep such a place secret. "Secret" is a relative term, as there are at least ten regulars who keep this secret. Probably more.

The river, squeezed between these ridges, fell in steps that left wadable fast water where it dropped and a couple deep runs you could easily cast across where it leveled. The high ridges made sunset come early in any season. As the shadows of old hemlocks fell on the water, a hatch of small caddisflies came off and a few rainbows began to sip obligingly.

The hole grew deeper as it progressed, and water soon reached my wader tops. I couldn't get behind the rainbows to fish upstream, at least, not without swimming. So I lengthened my leader and tied on a size-sixteen caddis with the intention of drifting it down to the fish.

The water flowed slowly in this part of the pool, so any fish would have a good look. Still, no crosscurrents created drag allowing me to give them a reasonable presentation by throwing a little slack in my leader.

As the shadows lengthened, more fish began to rise, and I picked up a few pint-sized rainbows. The largest was about ten inches with bright colors. They were scrappy and aggressive and made up for their lack of heft with a little extra bravado. It reminded me of throwing foam spiders to a bed of bluegill, each fish a joy unto itself.

After drying the caddis from catching the latest rainbow, I targeted another sipper and sent the fly in his direction. The leader had just enough curves to have time for the fly to drift past the fish before drag set in. The rainbow sipped it and turned to run.

This one was smaller than the rest, probably six inches or so. I say probably because I never landed him.

As the fish cut across the pool to escape, it dove and suddenly felt heavier. I lifted my rod tip, but it wouldn't budge. I thought the rainbow had run through a snag and then my line began to move.

Clearly, something larger had eaten my fish.

The brown trout—Why is it always a brown trout that creates havoc?—rose to the surface and held in the slow current. Even in the shadows, I recognized what had latched on.

Slowly, he turned and began moving downstream.

At this point, it dawned on me that I was likely still hooked to the rainbow. Unless the brown swallowed the small fish, I'd have no firm connection to the bigger one, so I didn't press the fight. Time could work in my favor.

The brown kept angling away heading downriver. That's when the trailing end of my fly line passed through the tip of my rod and the orange backing began to follow it.

Such an event is rare enough on mountain streams that I paused to look. I'd not seen my entire fly line leave my reel lately and it felt odd. Clearly this was a redletter day to see my backing due to a fish I had no hook in pulling out my line.

I saw no way to follow the fish short of swimming, so I stayed put and tested my luck. The backing peeled out slowly. Since the trout probably wasn't hooked, all he likely felt was resistance from the line. He was out for a leisurely stroll while he had dinner at my expense.

I continued to fight the trout, or should I say, guide him gingerly as best I could. A windfall on the left bank would be a problem if he found it. I doubted he would head into the fast water below to run, but the best place for a long fight was the middle of the pool. All I had to do was convince him to swim there and stay.

I decided to start regaining my line.

The old trout appeared interested in hanging onto his dinner and came when I applied pressure. With every shake of his head, I expected the caddis to come sliding out. Still, it was getting late, and I was running out of options.

The old brown stopped in the middle of the pool about twenty feet away. I leaned on him a little to get him moving again and he slowly rose, his back making a crease in the surface film.

We held like this for some time. The fish drifted from side to side, occasionally bulldogging his head to shake loose whatever was slowing him down. I kept trying to coax him upstream of me where I would be pulling the hook back into the corner of his mouth rather than out the front. He had settled in, however, and I had no way to get below him.

Then I felt what I dreaded most, a slipping of the line while I could see the fish was stationary. Only about twenty feet of water lay between us but at this point it might as well have been an ocean.

My fly slid out and the brown sank back into the pool. He had managed to both eat the rainbow and dodge the hook. Dinner on me with no movie afterward.

Now almost dark, I reeled in my line and hooked the caddis in the keeper ring. In the fading light my walk out of the woods was measured as I followed the trail back to the riffle where I crossed. The night air brought a humid chill with it and the sounds of night birds. An owl announced his claim on this territory as his to hunt.

Once back on the road, I bumped into another fisherman, one of the regulars who knew the hole. He guessed where I'd been fishing so we exchanged reports.

"Do any good?" he asked.

"Some small rainbows," I answered. "How about you?"

"Much the same. Nothing of any size. Did you see the big brown?"

"He ate one of my rainbows," I replied.

The fisherman chuckled. "I had him hit a streamer in there last week, so that doesn't surprise me. Knock-down-drag-out fight. Didn't land him but he looked to go twenty-five inches. He's a slab."

"Well, with a size-sixteen caddis in the fish he ate, I don't think I even stuck him."

We waved goodnight and headed to our trucks.

The drive out was slow and winding. Fish that get away often dwell longer in our memories than the ones we catch. My mind rehashed the fight, tried alternate scenarios, and let them play out while I mechanically followed the road.

Big fish on mountain streams deserve these places in our thoughts, as they are few and far between. Even more rare are white squirrels, feeding hellbenders, and a brown trout that takes you into your backing without even sticking him with a hook.

Maybe next time I'll get him to be the fish that eats the fly. There's always a next time.

Gone with
the Wind Knot

Suppose someone walked up to you in a bar and handed you a limp rope and asked you to tie a knot in the far end, thirty feet away, using nothing but the movement of the rope. If you could, they would pick up your tab. You would likely tell them to go stuff an otter and get back to knocking the froth off a cold one.

Yet we manage to do exactly that with our fly lines, and we call them wind knots, as if the wind is to blame. Either that, or wood fairies are playing pranks on us during our backcasts.

In any event, we often find ourselves with an extra knot in our leaders when we break at the end of the day. When it arrived and how it got there seems a mystery.

Fishermen who understand such knots generally ascribe them to tailing loops. The cause of tailing loops varies with the fisherman you ask. Some pin them on timing, either your forward cast starts too soon or you finish your cast too soon. Others blame the speed of the cast and an uneven casting stroke. Others suggest wind knots result from slack in the cast introduced by incorrect rod movement before the cast.

In his book *Casting with Lefty Kreh*, Lefty says, "Almost all tailing loops occur when the rod tip speeds up and stops in a straight path, and the line collides with itself."

Lefty goes on to describe causes of tailing loops and ways to prevent them. Yet the ability to stop doing something I don't know I'm doing eludes me.

I have noticed a few conditions that contribute to wind knots, at least on my line. Two flies seem more capable of tying knots than any single fly. Likewise, their knot tying propensity increases when at least one of them is weighted. Throw in a split shot and I'm convinced they could weave a pair of mittens or, as they actually do sometimes, a bird's nest.

Wind knots might be less of a problem if they were harmless. I would even forgive them if they picked up minute debris on the water surface that I would have to shake loose from time to time. Instead, these insidious culprits manage to cut the breaking strength of an otherwise straight leader by half.

Sometimes, it matters.

For instance, a couple years back I found myself by good chance in Scotland with a day free from the normal headaches of work. I contacted a couple local guides and found one who could put me on the River Tweed. Henceforth, I will refer to him as Ghillie.

When he picked me up, no clouds could be seen in any direction despite the reputation Scotland has for fickle weather.

"Nice day," I commented to start the conversation as he drove.

"I'd prefer a little rain," said Ghillie. "We haven't had a drop in three weeks."

This was about the time I noticed the same castle going by on our left side for the second or third time. Nothing generates confidence in a guide like getting lost.

As we left the city, sheep began to dot the hillsides like cotton balls with charcoal noses. The villages we passed through consisted of small homes and businesses clustered like flocks.

The anticipation continued to build as Ghillie talked about the River Tweed.

"The browns average three-quarters of a pound, but we see some three or four pounders. Grayling are a coarse fish here, but fun to catch. Something about that big fin on top seems to give them a little extra fight."

Ghillie had sufficiently pumped me up that when we arrived. I got booted up before he could string my rod.

Along the river, lambs frolicked in the fields. Unfamiliar flowers bloomed profusely. The water gurgled calmly and clearly, having not seen a rise from a rainstorm in three weeks.

To say the fishing was tough would be like describing James Bond as a flirt. One hour in and I was still fishless. Then it happened. Blue-winged Olives appeared in volumes that could qualify as a plague upon Egypt if the pharaoh wasn't a fly fisherman. But I was. So Ghillie started scrambling through his boxes for something that matched.

The Olives kept getting thicker. I swiped them out from inside my sunglasses. They landed on my nose and crawled on my ears. The back of Ghillie's waders sheltered the Olives from a breeze and they landed in such density it appeared they planned to carry him away.

Not a fish rose. Still, the Olives kept coming.

"In all my years," said Ghillie, and he had a lot of years, "I have never seen such a hatch."

On that note, we broke for lunch.

Ghillie handed me a longneck beer and I promptly covered the open end with my thumb. A couple other flies had begun to hatch, and the swarms hung over the river in small clouds. I ate smoked salmon on a roll, noting the irony that this was my first fish of the day.

My mind adjusted from wondering how many fish I would catch today to wondering if I was going to catch one.

We began to share theories on what was wrong with the fish in hope we could fix it. Ghillie's theory was too much sunshine and low water. It made sense. Brown trout like shadows and there were none.

I looked up at the sky into clouds of mayflies, the Olives joined by at least two other varieties. I had to think the prolific hatch had something to do with it. Spent Olives had begun to clog whirlpools and not a fish nose appeared.

"You know," I offered, "with all these bugs, the fish could just be stuffed. Especially if this goes on for days."

Ghillie nodded. "In that case, let's throw them something different."

He tied on a weighted nymph and a pink squirmy worm. So much for Scottish tradition.

Even the squirmy had no takers, swung Scottish-style or cast upstream and rolled into the hole American-style. We added weight, we took off weight, and we tried every part of the water column. Still not a fish.

By now, it was pushing three o'clock and my fishless day was moving toward an end. A small bank of clouds drifted across the sun and the first shadows of the day fell on the water. That's when it happened, a thump on my line, solid as a handshake.

I lifted my rod to set the hook and felt nothing. My line slid across the surface, and I looked at my leader. The bottom half was gone. No flies, no tippet, not even the adjoining knot.

I had never seen a leader break that far up, especially with no more force than the thump of a bite. The fish didn't run or yank my line—he just bit. The tug on my line had been minimal, just enough to know for sure it was a fish. And the break came in the split second before I tried to set the hook.

Ghillie studied my leader but had not a word to say. Given the point of the break, all I could figure was that I had a wind knot. Either that, or Scottish fairies clipped my line.

I leaned toward the wind knot theory as all the right conditions were there and I cannot prove fairies, or fish for that matter, exist in Scotland. I had been casting weighted nymphs. Between the nymphs, we did add a split shot. The leader was long enough with ample opportunity, as Lefty says, to collide on itself.

Finally, I had no other explanation for a leader to break above the tippet connection. In my mind, a wind knot it was.

So for my day on the River Tweed, I had a good beer, a nice salmon roll, and great scenery. Ghillie was entertaining and fine company. An epic Olive hatch has set the bar higher for what a hatch can look like.

After flailing for a day, swinging nymphs, and drifting dry flies, though, I had not one fish to show for it. I had the chance, but never landed the one that bit. He was gone with the wind knot.

Fly Fishing
for Suckers

Apparently, I have a knack for catching suckers on flies.

Having confessed this, it's not something I recommend unless you are willing to live with all that goes with it. You might try catching them when there is no one around, but if word gets out you will end up like me.

For starters, all my friends on Facebook want to see sucker pictures. These things have a face only their mothers could love. I'm always expected to do something ridiculous in the photo like faking a kiss, since the fish is already puckered up.

Once you establish a reputation as a sucker angler, everyone forgets that you only occasionally catch suckers and really do land a trout or redfish more frequently than you catch suckers. But most fishermen do that, so you become that sucker fisherman.

Should you be willing to live with all this, I will share my secrets for catching suckers on a fly.

To catch a sucker, first you have to fish where they are, which is on the bottom. That means you will be dredging with weighted nymphs, which some find demeaning. But if you only throw dry flies, you can forget about suckers. With their downturned mouths, they would have to turn upside down to feed.

Second, use a nymph that's small enough to go in a sucker's mouth. Even though they stay puckered up, anything bigger than a size-twelve nymph is less likely to be picked up.

Third, it's hard to match the hatch for what suckers feed on. My sucker nymph resembles moss. I don't know what suckers eat, but moss is my best guess.

I am often asked how to play a sucker. Hopefully, they mean the fish. It's not that difficult. They pull, you pull back. I don't remember ever losing one, especially if there were witnesses.

As far as the best tackle for suckers, I fish most of the time with an Orvis four-weight, and it doesn't seem overly insulted when I catch a sucker. I'm sure it catches grief when I put it back with my other rods, but it doesn't complain. Maybe other rods will.

When it's all said and done, I have mixed emotions about sucker fishing being my area of expertise. For instance, none of the rod companies have called me up for an endorsement. The tournament scene hasn't caught up to sucker fishing yet and sponsors are hard to sell. When I'm at the monthly Trout Unlimited meeting and everyone discusses their recent catches, I find myself prone to sit in silence and even lie sometimes about having gone fishing.

Also, carp fishermen look down on me from their low levels of self-esteem. They get articles and books written with stories about fishing in urban wastelands for carp but won't stoop to fly fishing for suckers. So why would anyone ever try to master sucker fishing on a fly rod?

Beats me. Probably better, though, than catching nothing.

The Colorado Years

Life will sometimes pause
and let us breathe.

Bob White, *Leaping Rainbow,* pencil on archival paper

Freedom

Freedom in the 1970s was a cooler full of New York strip steaks, enough gas money to fish my way home through Montana, and a trunk full of Coors beer. Behind all of this is a story.

THE JOB

If you've ever placed second in a job interview, then you probably don't have my fond memories of the experience. I had applied for a research position in Washington, DC, right out of college and placed second out of twenty-six. They told me this like it would cheer me up. The guy who came in ahead of me was a forestry classmate at Virginia Tech, so at least I knew he was deserving.

One of my other applications in the meantime had come back with an offer, so I accepted it instead. This offer was from a camp in Colorado that wanted me to run a hiking-and-fishing program for the summer with the grand remuneration of room, board, and $120 per month.

Shortly after I had accepted the hiking job, the research firm called back explaining they had received another grant and rather than interviewing everyone all over again, they decided to offer the job to me if I wanted it. I explained that I had accepted another position and my word was my bond and asked if I could start in October. They agreed and I was now sitting there thinking I had just gotten both jobs I wanted. I had four months to fish, hike, and see new country before the real world beckoned.

The trip out kicked off the adventure in fine style. West Virginia had just experienced floods that probably left fish in trees. I passed a church with the high-water mark on the steeple. The second night, I camped in Kansas and lightning drove me back into my 1967 Mustang. In the morning, all my gear was soaked, so I took out the tent poles, rolled it all into one big wad, and stuffed it in the trunk.

Arriving in Granby, Colorado, I learned that the winter had seen little precipitation, but forty inches of wet, heavy snow had fallen in May.

Trees had crashed and obstructed trails, so I had to hike every trail before taking guests out. Quickly, I acclimated to the elevation and broke in my new hiking boots.

The typical week was an introduction to the families on Monday with a short hike, an introductory fishing seminar where I asked if anyone wanted to fish, followed by five more days of scheduled hikes to lakes, peaks, and meadows. We alternated the hikes among the staff to avoid boredom and averaged about forty miles a week up and down mountains.

I fished on evenings and weekends. The seasonal rhythms of the waters and the progression from beaver ponds to creeks and high-mountain lakes, ending with headwaters of larger streams, created a schedule for finding fish. Mostly, it depended on the runoff and finding streams low enough to wade. The fish and I became fast friends.

THE DEAL

About midsummer, a family pulled into camp in a mobile home from Long Island, New York. From the first day, Mom, Dad, and two teen-aged boys were regulars on every activity we offered. As it turned out, they were traveling the country, looking for campgrounds the family enjoyed enough to stay in for some time, and then Dad hopped on a plane to Alaska to work on the pipeline. He worked about a month on and a couple weeks off, so I had the rest of the family as summer hikers.

Mom had grown up in Germany and told me stories about stealing food from American soldiers to support her family. She was six years old at the time. When she got chased, she dodged through railcars to escape.

After a week or so, I took the boys under wing to teach them the basics of fishing. We pestered the brookies in the camp beaver ponds until the boys had the hang of it. Before long, the family had developed a taste for trout.

I was repairing the camp spinning rods one evening when Mom wandered in and said she had a proposition for me. I braced myself until she added, "Here it is. We love trout better than anything. Even my husband loves trout. The boys catch just about enough to eat but I want you to stock my freezer before we drive away. I'll trade you pound for pound in New York strip steaks. How's that sound?"

After eating camp food and living on $120 per month, it sounded like manna from heaven with wild honey thrown in for good measure. I pretended to think about it before agreeing.

The shop I worked in for fishing-gear rentals and hiking sign-ups had a fridge with a freezer. I proceeded to fill it.

THE TRIP HOME

My summer job ended on Labor Day, which was the same day my favorite hiker family cranked up the mobile home to continue west. Dad was back behind the wheel, and good to her word, Mom met me with a cooler of steaks that started me drooling. I handed over the trout and waved as they drove off.

I cashed my last paycheck, got some tip money I hadn't expected, and drove into Granby. Back then, Coors didn't ship east, so my forestry buddies had left a standing order for Coors beer. I emptied the trunk's contents into the back seat, filled it back with Coors, stopped at the gas station to inflate the air shocks to compensate, and headed north.

If you have never been behind the wheel with nowhere to go for a month, not having to worry about your next job, and having a mobile feast in your car, then you may not understand the liberation I felt. No bills due, no homework, no deadlines. No place to be but where my curiosity led me.

My biggest challenge was deciding where to go. I knew Yellowstone would be a major milestone, but between Granby and southwest Montana, I waded creeks and beaver ponds throughout Colorado and Utah. If I saw a sign that sounded interesting, I turned and drove. I watched them excavate fossils in Dinosaur National Park, thinking the workers could become fossils themselves at the rate they worked.

Just before dark every day, I'd find a campground, preferably with grills so I could roast a steak. In a pinch, I'd crank up the backpack stove and eat fried steak. I started making a dent in the Coors supply.

I still remember the souvenir shops and T-shirts with slogans like, "Eat, drink, and be merry, for tomorrow you could be in Utah," or, "When a man tires of women, politics, and brandy, he can always hunt ducks." Actually, I bought that last one.

In Jackson Hole, I wandered around town until I heard a bunch of cowboys yelling and walked in hoping I wasn't stepping into the middle of a brawl. It was Sunday afternoon in the Silver Dollar Saloon and football was on a small TV up in the corner. The Cowboys were playing, and the cowboys were cheering for them. The building hadn't burned yet: that was a few years later. The bar top was covered in silver dollars coated with polyurethane or something like it to keep them from being stolen. The rumor was that someone had stolen the silver dollars and torched the bar to cover their tracks. I guessed there were a couple thousand silver dollars embedded in the bar.

I hung around Jackson Hole for a while, fishing and shooting photos of moose. I'd been photographing wildlife all summer and hadn't been around any moose in Colorado. I found a place on the map called Moose Pond and figured it was named that for a reason. I'm sharp that way.

I hiked in and set up along the pond to shoot photos of moose. The ranger had warned me that some of the bulls were getting aggressive, so I stayed careful. That is, until a passel of moose walked out behind me and herded me toward the pond where I skirted the edge, set up again, and took a few photos.

Still, none of these were big bull moose, so I hiked back to the car wondering where to go next. As soon as I saw the car, I realized a hefty bull was standing beside it. I walked around, framed him in front of the Tetons, and started rattling off film. It was that kind of summer.

The next stop was West Yellowstone, which I considered close enough to Heaven to see it from there. About two-thirds of the stores were fly shops and saloons. The other third didn't matter.

I can't remember much about the fish I caught, just that I caught some. Whenever I saw a stream that looked good or I recognized the name, I stopped and fished. I remember the last steak I grilled was the night before I left Yellowstone.

I went out through Cody, Wyoming, and stopped there for gas, asking what there was to do in town. The proprietor pointed to a gun museum that had old Winchesters, guns with coffee grinders in the stock, and pistols designed for gamblers so you could hide them in your hand with short barrels sticking between your fingers. They called them Knuckle Dusters because they left a powder stain and singed the hair off your knuckles.

Leaving the museum's gun section, I wandered into a wing of western art. Grizzlies holding dogs at bay and cowboys in action or contemplating the range, the images captured moments worth remembering. I soaked it in, knowing there was nowhere I'd rather be.

One mandatory stop for my trip was Dan Bailey's fly shop in Livingston, Montana. I'd worked in a hardware store in Virginia in high school and had been charged with ordering flies from Bailey's for our store. I'd heard that most of his fly-tyers were women and I wanted to see them at work. I imagined them all in the back like a knitting mill back home, cranking out boxes of bugs. The day I went in the store was quiet—probably fly season had a lull after the summer. So I admired all the fish and photos before heading on.

The rest of the trip was a blur. I skirted the Badlands and headed straight to my forestry buddies' houses. We spent evenings telling lies and drinking Coors. When I finally packed up and headed to DC for the real job, I was spent with the feeling that none of my time nor money was wasted, not a minute nor nickel. I'd spent all mine on a summer of freedom.

My place in DC was close enough to one of my forestry buddies that we often met to fish. Buck and I were sitting in a boat reliving my tales out west, probably for the third or eighth time, when he interrupted and asked, "If it was really that good, why don't you do it again?"

I thought about the job in DC. and the trout in the Rockies and made one of those fateful dares. "I will if you will."

And we did.

Coldcocked

My introduction to beaver-pond ducks came with a camera in my hand. I shot photos for wildlife magazines back then, which allowed me to pay for my outdoor habits. I was sneaking up on a beaver pond one June afternoon, figuring it was a good place to see beavers. At least, it seemed like the right place to look.

In my early photography days, I shot Kodachrome 64 in a Nikkormat body with a zoom lens that cost more than a good shotgun. Buck, my buddy, was a better photographer than I was, but his preference was wildflowers with a macro lens. We never got in each other's way unless my wildlife started eating his vegetation.

One reason I had no beaver photos is that beavers were elusive and I'm a bumbler. The only one I had seen on this string of ponds had slipped up behind me while I cast flies to brookies. He saw me first and slapped his tail so hard it sounded like a rifle shot. My bladder control was better in those days, so the only side effect was extra jittering action in my retrieve. The brookies liked it.

Anyway, on this sunny June afternoon, I crept up on the beaver dam, keeping low and out of sight. When I rose enough to see over, I found no beavers working, but a shiny greenhead sat at the far end of the pond. I clicked off a few picturesque shots but had learned long before that duck photos need action. Buck agreed to go around, come up from the back side, and flush the drake my way.

Everything started out according to plan. The mallard popped off the pond and hightailed it straight at me. When he was filling up my zoom, I stood to make him flare in the sunshine. He did, showing that pale underbelly like faded-white long johns under a flannel shirt.

I must have surprised him a lot because he veered straight into a lodgepole pine and fell to the ground coldcocked. I looked quickly around for either a vet to resuscitate him or a wildlife officer to lock me up. But the duck stood, got his bearings, and took off only slightly worse for wear.

I thought little about the beaver-pond mallards until September rolled around. After Labor Day, the summer fishermen migrate home to their jobs and leave the local trout to the local fishermen. My favorite fall stream drained that valley of beaver ponds, and in the late season, the water trickled and fluttered over the rocks as the ponds rationed what was left.

Colorado skies in the fall are bluest when the aspens go to gold, the scenery local gift shops worship. The aspens weren't quite there yet, but you could imagine it. I was standing mesmerized by the melancholy of the fall season, comfortably cool, water gurgling, shadows lengthening across the aspens, when a pair of wings whistled past my ear. I watched a mallard hen flapping for all she was worth toward the beaver ponds. Two drakes came right behind her. I realized then that this headwater was the mallard's exit route south when the beaver ponds froze. I marked my mental calendar for the opening day of duck season.

The early duck season came after the high country had regular frosts. The aspens had peaked, and the forest floor became the gold in those hills. I decided to camp nearby, both to shorten the drive and to turn what could be a bust of a duck hunt into a backwoods experience.

I cooked a late meal of beef stew over a one-burner Coleman backpack stove and chased it down with a Coors that made the night air colder. The stars moved in close when the fire died down. Astronomers must be born on mountaintops.

Just before dawn, I woke to yips coming up the valley. Not too close, but a good pack of coyotes making a last round before the sun rose.

Coyotes were plentiful here as I'd seen the year before. Some friends had asked me to take them on an overnight camping trip and they brought their friends with them. The group grew until we had about fifteen college kids on an adventure. I walked them up to a high meadow with an established fire ring. We sat up late, told stories, and slept under the stars. When it came time to sleep, I moved to the outer edge where the trees met the grass.

At about four in the morning, an owl landed on the branch above my head. I woke to hoots and lay still, watching his silhouette against the night sky. The moon was setting but still gave off a pale light. The fire had died to an orange glow, but I could make out the lumps of campers around the fire.

Then I heard the yips and howls at the far end of the meadow. Coyotes, vocal and coming our way, on the hunt. As they came to the edge of camp, I expected them to circle around and keep going or spook and reverse themselves. Instead, they went silent and slipped through camp between the sleeping bags. I could see their bodies as they blocked the campfire glow, maybe a dozen of them. All they did was pass on, and once out of camp, they began their yipping and howling again. Not a camper woke. My owl waited one last minute and sailed down the meadow in the opposite direction.

I told none of the campers about the coyotes.

My own coyotes here in my duck-hunting camp stayed farther away. It wasn't their presence that made me reluctant to rise but the frost on my sleeping bag. Greeting that first bite of cold coming out of a warm bag takes mental fortitude, or in my case, a personal bribe of hot coffee. I made the leap, started the Coleman burner, and packed up.

Wading the trout stream in the dark proved simple enough. The riffles held no surprises. I picked a split in the headwater on a small island that would give me a place to hide behind some low brush, just high enough to break my outline. I dropped four decoys out in the seams of flow where a duck might feed. The current made them swim easily side to side. I faced upstream toward the beaver ponds and waited.

As the sun hit it, the frost on the banks melted and rose as wisps of fog. The dry air sucked the moisture as it danced in the beams of light. Then it was gone.

Duck hunters call these bluebird days, as the sky offers nothing but sunshine. The sun continued higher, and I sat watching the river and my decoys, thinking maybe I should have fished instead.

Mallards are sometimes late sleepers. The first one came down the river, hell-bent for its feeding grounds downstream. The drake gave me plenty of notice and planned to pass on my left. I put a bead on him before he made the cut and he fell in front of me.

In the next twenty minutes, all of the beaver ponds flushed their ducks and they came to me. Drakes and hens, local summer ducks, all headed downstream. I picked the greenheads out of the small bunches, and in this tight, the shooting was decisive. Either I missed or the duck dropped cleanly. By eight thirty, it was over. I sat quietly watching the river trickle by, three greenheads lined up at my feet.

I packed up about nine thirty, figuring I'd head out before the fishermen showed up and deduced that I'd been shooting trout. Driving home, I had that feeling you get after a really good meal when you've eaten just enough. The hunting had been a pleasant surprise, satisfaction after playing a hunch, and I had shot all the ducks I wanted.

Once home, I stowed the gear and began to pluck the ducks. One of the greenheads had an odd little knot on his head. Upon closer inspection, it looked like he had flared into a lodgepole pine and been coldcocked. Or maybe I'd just caught him there with a pellet.

It's hard to say.

Skinny-Dipping
with Cutties

When I need to divert my mind from tasks at hand, it readily goes back to a time when my legs were stronger, my wallet thinner, and beer was judged by how cold it was. Those were my hiking-guide days in Colorado when I could be convinced to take anyone on a hike anywhere as long as water and fish were part of the itinerary.

A family came into our YMCA camp one day asking me to take them to a high-mountain lake they had found on a map. The backpack shop in town assured them it was seven miles in and the trail easy to follow. I had hiked the first few miles of the trail before but had always taken a different fork that led to a larger lake. At least I knew where to start.

The family had hiked with me earlier in the week and seemed fit enough for the trip. Dad and his two teenagers were getting used to the altitude, so we agreed to go on Friday.

The surprise came on Friday morning when we were to set out. New to their group for just this trip was Mom, a farm lady who assured me she was up to it. Still, she had yet to go on a hike. Ours would start at nine thousand feet above sea level and go to eleven thousand feet. Her four days in camp weren't enough for her to acclimate.

I'd not bothered to check the distance on the topo map, partly because there were too many switchbacks to allow an educated guess. The reason there were so many switchbacks is that the last three miles were up.

To spare you the play-by-play, we arrived at the lake at about two that afternoon. Mom was spent and I was concerned we could turn this one around in a day. While they rested, I scouted the lakes.

A large upper lake nestled against the mountain at timberline, so the far side was open rocks and cliffs while the near side ran into the pine forest. The pines provided sufficient shade to preserve snowbanks, offering refrigeration for perishables.

The lower lake was small and shallow with about a hundred feet of creek connecting the two. With the water crystal clear, the bottom was visible almost throughout the lower lake. Cutthroat cruised the shoreline actively feeding. They had all the behaviors of fish hungry after a long winter and still catching up. They mostly fed subsurface, and I made a mental note. Since I'd not brought a rod along the decision to come back was made already.

My farm family looked either ready to go or be helicoptered out. We got Mom standing and Dad started pushing her down the trail. She kept picking up one foot after the other to plod down the mountain. We would stop frequently, give Mom a breather, and then coax her back up with the lie that it wasn't far now.

The good news is that we survived and reached our vehicles just before dark. The hike measured ten miles each way instead of the seven promised. Still, once back at camp I put out the word that I'd found a new lake with fish. Those with the weekend off showed up at my door; by morning four of us met with packs and rods ready to go.

Our camp staff consisted mostly of college kids looking for a summer adventure, so a pack trip to a remote lake with a potential fish dinner was the payoff most had come for. We somehow wedged four packs and people into my 1967 Mustang and drove to the trailhead.

We got a late start due to stopping for a few provisions and not being in a hurry anyway. So our mountain hike occurred during the summer afternoon heat. With forty-pound packs, our backs were soon wet with sweat. The two guys and the girl ahead of me talked incessantly about how good it would feel to take a swim upon arrival.

By the time we engaged the switchback sections, they had decided to just drop their packs at the edge of the lake along with their clothes and take a running jump. One thing they had not factored in was that most of the water from this lake came from snowmelt. Snow may melt just above freezing but it doesn't instantly become bathwater. I kept it to myself that this lake didn't even thaw until late June.

As we hiked, they kept talking up the swim. I assured them that I would be content catching dinner on the lower lake.

The trail ended at a site good for tents between the two lakes. As promised, I grabbed my gear and went down to the lower lake while they dropped everything, including clothes, in a mad dash to the upper.

I was close enough to hear twigs breaking underfoot as they ran. In my mind, I could picture them in midair, over the water in one unified leap, and then I heard three splashes in unison.

The pause while the three were underwater made the stillness foreboding, like a moment from an old horror film. I could envision them paddling madly back toward the surface looking to escape the grasp of the icy water.

Seconds later, their screams came in unison, just as their splashes had. If the water's cold enough, three people can learn the same primal language simultaneously.

The fish delivered on their earlier promise. We ate cutties for dinner over a fire in the dark. Spent, we slept under the stars, and I used the sun as an alarm so I could catch our breakfast.

The cutthroat, having lived the winter under the ice, seemed tolerant of any pattern so long as I didn't spook them. Soft hackles just under the surface and small nymphs both worked. I don't remember changing flies unless one became worn. The fish all ran ten to fourteen inches and this lower lake sported fish to the point they became competitive for food.

We had trout for breakfast, and no one complained of having the same meal twice. All of us had to work the next day, so by midmorning we broke camp and started hiking.

Since then, I've been back to these lakes twice. In both cases, the fish cooperated as before, and our meals consisted mainly of trout. Whenever we timed our trip to catch the lakes soon after the thaw, the fish acted like they had not eaten since the fall.

Our provisions improved on these latter trips. Premixed omelets replaced the oatmeal. Late-night beverages moved a bit more upscale. And having heard the stories from earlier trips, none of my companions braved the cold water for a swim.

Still, when my mind drifts back to those lakes now, my first thought is of me threading an old fiberglass fly rod and smiling while waiting to hear three splashes and the subsequent screams.

The Fish of
a Lifetime

The final weeks of the Columbine bloom run out in the higher elevations of Colorado from mid- to late June. Suckers spawn during those last weeks, moving up creeks flush with snowmelt. Following those suckers are lake trout out of the depths where, for a period, they can be caught in shallow water.

Back in the late 1970s, I'd befriended a local fishing guide who tipped me off to the timing and whereabouts of this spawning-and-feeding movement. A stream between two lakes offered the suckers spawning grounds, and a point at the mouth of the stream was a prime place to cast to incoming fish. My goal was to catch one of these lakers on a fly rod.

When the guide took clients out to fish for these lakers, he usually put cut-sucker bait on the bottom and let the lakers find it. If the fisherman he was guiding got restless, he gave them a jig tied with mallard feathers on a lead head. Either of these on heavy spinning tackle offered a fair match to these fish. My fly rod, on the other hand, skewed the advantage well in favor of the fish.

The sucker spawn was tailing out on my last attempt from the point at the mouth of the creek. The Columbine bloom had passed its peak, confirming an end to this phase of the season. I cast large streamers, working the lake inward and up the creek for twenty yards or so before returning to repeat the route. My earlier attempts had been fruitless and this morning was following the pattern.

Upstream a couple hundred yards, a small public campground sat next to the stream and its inhabitants routinely walked over to cast salmon eggs in hopes of catching rainbow trout for supper. A few fishermen were scattered along the stream today, spaced evenly up to the bend in the creek.

The closest to me was a fellow cut from the mold of Paulie, Rocky's brother-in-law, from the 1976 movie. He was the same height and build, wore a nylon windbreaker against the morning chill, and sported a porkpie hat. He had bushy sideburns and the look of a man who worked with his hands. His signature feature was a cigar chewed or smoked to less than half its original length.

Whenever I fished my section up closer to him, I'd watch the way fishermen do to see if he was picking up anything. He fished with a Zebco spincast outfit, one of the shorter ones that came standard with light line.

Having been flailing the water from daylight to midmorning, my thoughts were turning toward breakfast. I made a deal with myself to fish one more lap and quit if I had no bites, the fisherman's equivalent of "just one more cast."

As I approached Paulie and began to wrap up my fly gear, I noticed that his rod was bent. He may have been on the fish for a while, as I'd been distracted by fishing myself, but whatever he was onto had some weight. The tight line cut a V in the water where it entered and throbbed when the fish moved.

I decided to watch.

The fish held in the middle of the stream; whatever line it conceded it quickly took back. My guess was Paulie had hooked a laker on a small hook and a salmon egg.

Paulie would lean back on his rod to guide the fish to the bank. It would swerve in momentarily and provide a little hope, then with a tilt of its body glide back out to midstream. Paulie may have held the rod, but the lake trout was in control.

I figured he was one run to the lake from this fight being over. Paulie must have guessed the same. That's when he yelled for help at the top of his lungs, stretching it out as if falling off a cliff and screaming until he hit bottom.

I hustled up the creek and stood beside him for a moment. The fish held in waist-deep water. I had on chest waders so in theory I could reach the fish if it didn't move. But that was a big if. I wanted Paulie to understand this could go badly.

"I can wade out to him," I offered, "and maybe get his head in this net. But if he spooks and turns to the lake, he'll break you off."

"That's fine," replied Paulie. "I can't get him closer to the bank. I don't have a choice. Do it."

So I slowly waded in to avoid spooking the fish. The closer I got, the bigger it looked. Also, the water was just inches below the top of my waders. If the fish swerved out even a little, he'd be out of reach.

My net seemed to shrink as I positioned it ahead of the fish. Clearly it would be inadequate to scoop the laker, but it might just hold its head. I moved the net slowly toward the laker's head and simultaneously grabbed the fish in front of its tail.

The grip on the tail felt like grabbing a weight-lifter's wrist. Solid, it was my best grip. With a net over the head and a hand on the tail, I brought the fish toward me. That's when it woke up.

The lake trout, thrashing like a bucket of eels, seemed to go in all directions at once. Water flew from the flapping fish. Long and lean, it flexed in the middle, then responded by going the other direction with its head and tail. Waders or not, I was getting drenched. It was all I could do to hold on.

I still had a firm grasp of the tail but the laker was chomping through the fabric net. At this point, I could feel his head sliding forward as it expanded the opening. Soon it would punch through.

I had no choice but to move as quickly as possible. Sloshing toward the bank, I made haste, but timing would prove critical. That's when I felt the laker break through the net. I was still eight to ten feet from the bank.

In an instant it was going to be over one way or another. I rolled the squirming fish back onto the crook of my elbows, flexed them in to cradle the laker, but I could tell I wouldn't be able to hold him. So I straightened my arms and flung the fish as far up the bank as I could. Paulie, having watched intently from the sidelines, fell on it like a wrestler and had it pinned. He lay there huffing and puffing until I walked out.

Once the fish was subdued, Paulie brought out a scale and weighed it at an even seventeen pounds. I scrambled back to my camera and snapped a few shots. Paulie stood with the mountains behind him, a char over half his length in one hand, and a cigar chewed to a nub in the corner of his mouth.

That lake trout probably hangs on a wall in Paulie's house and the story of the catch gets bigger each year. Perhaps that's the way it should be with fishing stories. The fish of a lifetime should last a lifetime.

Pondering Deer Stuff

Not actual deer stuff,
but stuff about deer.

Bob White, *The Wolf*, pencil on archival paper

Hunting
with KP

Henny Youngman is credited with the lines, "You have the Midas touch. Everything you touch turns into a muffler."

He could have been talking about KP.

KP was a contradictory sort. Whenever he bungled a task, he told on himself and laughed along. This happened often, so when the guys in the maintenance shop rested and wanted an entertaining tale, they turned to KP. The first story I heard from him when we met involved target practice with a .22 rifle.

"I put a paper target on my woodshed wall to try out my new rifle," he began. "I braced myself on the arms of a chair on my front porch. On my first shot, I hit the target and heard a ping. That didn't make sense, so I did it again. Another ping."

KP continued to shoot and continued to hear pings. He would listen and try to figure out why a wooden shed would make such a sound when you shot it.

His story went on like this until he had emptied the .22 rifle magazine and walked out to check on his target. Satisfied with his pattern, he then walked into the shed to discover the source of the pinging noise.

"I guess I should have done that earlier," said KP. "I had a nice set of wire hubcaps hanging on the inside wall and now one of them was shot all to hell and back."

The guys in the shop laughed and muttered about how they didn't think they would have told that story on themselves. Probably few would. But KP not only wrote the book on himself, he also let everyone read it. The only exception is one story that only he and I know. This is it.

We were both taking up bowhunting at that time and trying to figure out the sport with equipment cobbled together from the local hardware store. We mangled straw bales with broadheads until the bales fell apart. Scouting in the late summer heat, we found trails, built blinds, and got ready for deer season.

Opening day came at the end of a torrential rain. Creeks ran out of their banks and into the woods. Roads into hunting areas rutted to impassability. Our local brand of mud, isinglass, absorbed water until it glazed over as slick as otter snot. On a damp slope, a person could hardly stand on it, much less walk. When a truck with snow tires ran through isinglass, the mud filled the spaces between the lugs until the surface was coated in slick ungripping mud, driving like bald tires.

Since conventional wisdom had led us to believe the best blinds were far into the woods, we faced a long opening-day hike down a washed-out logging road. We left KP's truck at the pavement and hoofed it in.

The first obstacle we met was a creek we could usually cross by stepping on stones. It raged into the trees, and our ford where the roadbed crossed looked like someone had kicked open a splash dam to float timber out.

KP and I studied the situation until I spoke.

"You want to go upstream and me downstream and hunt this side of the creek? I don't think we'll get to our blinds today."

He nodded and ambled off in search of a hunting spot.

I eased along the creek looking for a place to hunt or cross. This was new ground to me as we had been going farther in to scout. All tracks and deer sign had been swept clean in the downpour, so the most evidence I could see were splits in the vegetation where deer had worn out some space.

Downstream just a couple hundred yards, I looked up from the trail to see a posted sign marking private property and the end of public federal land where I could hunt. Having not scouted this close to the truck, I'd not seen it before. I decided to reconvene with KP and hunt upstream of him.

Walking back to the roadbed where we split up, I stopped and listened momentarily. I could hear nothing over the sound of rushing water, the usual gurgle now a soft roar.

Suddenly, I caught a glimpse of movement rushing straight at me. Contrasting images of bright white and camo green flashed before me in a headlong calamity coming directly toward the spot where I stood. KP ran and jumped, all the while looking back over his shoulder. He carried his bow in one hand and alternated waving his free hand behind him and reaching to pull his camo pants up to his knees so he could run, or at least shuffle at high speed.

Seeing someone running in stark terror directly toward you creates an impulse to draw a weapon or break into a mad dash so you're at least in front of the other victim. I expected to see the guys from *Deliverance* coming directly behind KP, brandishing long knives as they drooled through toothless grins. Or perhaps a lumbering bear trailing her cubs, growling and in a lather.

The commotion kept coming and I held my ground, frozen. In the end, it was only KP.

He continued shuffling, bumbling, fanning, and jumping until he reached the roadbed where I stood in awe of a scene so out of the norm, I had no words. His face reflected surprise when he saw me, then regret when he realized I saw him.

The camo I had seen were his shirt and bunched-up pants, while the flashes of white were from a fanny that rarely saw daylight. Contrasting colors such as these look neon in somber woods. His posterior could have been flashing on and off and been no more visible.

He handed me his bow for a moment while he modestly pulled his pants back up.

I didn't even know where to start. So I asked the question that originally brought me here.

"The land downstream is posted. Anywhere up here to hunt?"

"I don't know," said KP. "I didn't get that far."

Then I got to the point.

"What was that all about?"

KP looked at his boots and rearranged rocks in the roadbed. He bought as much time as his distraction could purchase and then answered.

"After we split up, I had to answer nature's call."

"Not the hunting kind?"

"No, the other kind," said KP. "I thought I'd go near the roadbed to keep my scent out here. So I dropped my pants and squatted only to discover I was over a yellow jacket's nest."

"Guess they didn't like that," I offered in consolation.

"Not a bit. They attacked."

KP was clearly in discomfort, physically and mentally, still stung with embarrassment and perhaps yellow jackets, so I asked.

"Any stings?"

"At least four."

"Hmmm." I had no medicinal solutions or home remedies to offer. Back then, the common treatment was wet tobacco or baking soda. I had neither.

"You want to go?" I asked. The weather had blown all our scouting and KP looked like he had enjoyed all he could stand.

"I think so."

The walk back to his truck took a while, mostly being uphill and back and forth across ruts that took out the middle of the road and weaved between the ditches. The mud caked on our boots made each step a chore. KP had started to scratch at places that gave me clues where his stings were, trying to do it when I wasn't looking. Just the thought of yellowjacket stings in remote regions made me wince.

At one pause, KP glanced over at me with a curious look. Finally, the question came out.

"You're not going to tell the guys at the shop, are you?"

I grinned, he grinned back, and we started walking.

Should any of the guys at the shop read this, they will not doubt a word of it, as they know KP. And KP, you should know that I kept your secret for over forty years. In the end, that's the best I could do.

Hunting in the Haunted House

Our favorite deer stand fifty years ago was in a haunted house. Every opening day, it yielded one nice buck, and over time, we came to understand both its allure to deer and its haunts.

As I recall, we had permission to hunt from a distant cousin or some other obscure family connection. Few people walked that far to shoot a deer and then try to drag it back out. The timber had been cut during the Depression, so even the logging roads had grown back in hardwoods. Their ruts ran through the trees to guide us to the house in the dark.

The abandoned house was in a steady state of collapse. The roof on one end fell to an angle and almost reached the ground. Rusted barrel hoops and farm tools littered the yard and a few ornamental bushes past their prime clung to the side of the house.

The steadiest part of the structure was the chimney, and that's where the stand was built. Over the years, the chimney had filled with sticks and leaves. After we put a makeshift ladder against it and climbed up, we could tamp down the leaves and stand waist-deep inside the chimney. From that vantage, a hunter could watch between two ridges of hardwoods, both marked by scrapes and rubbed trees to let us know another buck had staked this as his territory.

The story behind the haunting grew fuzzy over time. What I recall was that a couple and their two children lived there in the 1920s. With a natural spring at the edge of the yard and some measure of prosperity encouraging them to build, the family had made a home. Then, hard times produced desperate actions. Whether they were murdered and robbed or just gave up wasn't clear.

What was clear was that it was never a quiet house to hunt. There were noises.

You never heard them so much during the day. The world was louder then, with crows overhead making raucous sounds and squirrels chattering in the hickories or shuffling leaves in search of nuts they had stashed when they were plentiful.

In the hours before daylight, however, you could hear the house as if something lived in it. Things moved. Boards splintered and groaned. Footsteps of unknown sizes crept across the old floors where no person could stand and walk. Glassless windows framed empty blackness, doorways for what crept inside. When the night lies engulfed by shadows, sounds become images in our imagination.

Tales play back through the mind. Ghost stories are told as fact by our ancestors, so a house with a bad ending could easily host a few apparitions. You only had to hear them walking to believe.

Standing in the chimney in that last hour before sunrise, a hunter could be forgiven for being edgy, for easing the safety back and forth once to check its position. If a breeze chilled the back of the neck, one might question if it was just the wind. If not for the promise of the buck that also made the haunted house part of its territory, one might reasonably forgo such a stand.

As we grew into our late teens, the indestructible years, the house had a particular draw to it, a test of sorts. Almost like an initiation, we wanted to hunt it to prove our steadfastness in the face of superstition. And as much as we enjoyed the mystery of it, we wanted to unravel it at the same time.

So finally, we took on the house itself. We crawled over it, peered into it, and looked under it. We waited for a sunny afternoon when even the shadows retreated.

Not much that hadn't been picked clean by human scavengers was inside. We found a few zinc lids to blue jars, gray with time. An old bed frame lay mangled where the roof had fallen on it. A pantry was jammed shut from the shifting foundation, anything inside long since spoiled.

The foundation rested on top of stones stacked evenly to keep the house level. The beams for the floor sat about eighteen inches above the ground. These beams, made from oak and chestnut, might outlast even the chimney.

It was in that eighteen-inch crawl space where our mysteries lived. The dirt remained bare, but a coat of dust on top of packed clay recorded every track. It had the look of a wildlife superhighway. Deer tracks pocked the dust where no deer could walk, only crawl. Smaller tracks crisscrossed larger ones until no line could be traced in the maze of prints. We followed them on our bellies to where they were thickest, trying to understand what brought these animals under the house.

Then we found it.

A small room on the end concentrated all the activity beneath it. Its floorboards were chewed into splinters as if animals were eating the wood itself for sustenance.

The room above had been where they cured hams after killing the fall hog. Heavily salted, the hams had oozed fat and salt into the flooring until the house itself had become one big lick. Year after year, the family had added seasoning to the floor until they left it for the wild animals to consume.

In the cover of darkness, deer crawled beneath the house for the salt. Field mice ran the floors in search of scarce nutrients. The predators followed the mice, doing their hunting in the cover of darkness.

In that final hour before sunrise on opening day, the house came to life. The meager deer population concentrated around this wooden salt block. The haunting sounds echoed from the pattering of small feet on old boards and into our imaginations, ever so often laced with a squeal as a predator captured its prey.

Breezes once again became merely the wind, as understanding shed light on superstitions. No one checked their safety anymore, except with the intent to confirm it was in the proper position when the buck finally stepped out.

The Deer Who
Wore Camo

In my youth, Hemingway had convinced a generation of us to be cold and hard. Hunting glory only rained on the strong. Wilderness beckoned the worthy. Success came to those who suffered quietly.

So when deer-hunting season approached, my buddy and I drove as far into the wild mountains as our car would take us. We walked miles before we began to scout. We found abusive terrain to climb, and then we looked for impenetrable cover. We built our deer stands there.

With any luck, our season would be blessed by miserable weather. Sleet would be nice, though a cold drizzle would be more painful, especially if carried by a northeast wind that hadn't warmed since it left Newfoundland.

One year, when we built our stands in such a place and the weather blew in almost as prescribed, it coincided with the last week of deer season.

The drizzle began before first light. Walking in by flashlight felt like threading our way through ominous gargoyles, as the trees loomed with their waving arms overhead. The mountain was so steep goats would have used a handrail.

We split up near the end of the trail to go to our stands. Mine overlooked a sharp drop with a white oak grove at the bottom where acorns might entice a buck to step out for lunch. My buddy's stand poked out from a rhododendron thicket with branches interwoven tighter than Grandma's knitting.

Once in my stand, the drizzle searched for the dry spot behind my neck, the way water swirls before finding the drain. A shift in the wind helped it, so I spent the rest of the day cold and hard. Hemingway would have approved.

Behind the low, thick clouds the sun moved undetected. Time had no marker, and the day was scored only by events. A gobbler foraged in the leaves, a squirrel climbed the tree my stand was in, and scratchy-throated ravens called from inside the clouds. Then, late in the day, a rifle shot cracked once from where only my buddy could have fired.

At dark, I moved to the trail where we had split up, expecting to find him dragging a deer. Instead, he was standing there waiting.

"Miss?" I asked in typical Hemingway dialogue, wasting no words.

"No, dressed him and hung him for the night. A four-pointer." I thought I heard teeth chattering. "Thought that given the terrain we'd pack him out tomorrow in quarters."

"Fine," I agreed, handling my end of the entire conversation in just two words.

Once we started out, the drizzle stopped, partly because the clouds dropped. We were in them or in fog equivalent to them. It was now night and the darkness seemed to absorb our flashlights. Unable to see the trail, we followed the contour instead.

Somewhere along the way, I stopped to look around and hide the fact that I was sucking wind. My heart thumped like a drum in a St. Patrick's Day parade. My buddy's shiver was almost imperceptible, like hand signals under the table at a poker game.

I leaned against an old chestnut oak as casually as I knew how. "Shouldn't we be on the main trail by now?" I asked, forgetting my word count.

"It should be just ahead," he replied, with only a crack of doubt.

Thirty minutes later, I found myself leaning against the same tree. Seeing that tree again was like picking up yesterday's newspaper.

I asked the obvious question. "You sure this is the way out?"

He noticed my tree, the same one from earlier.

"This has to be the right ridge and it has to be the right direction."

"So why did we circle?" I asked.

"Must be a mountaintop."

I grunted, having used up my words.

We dropped down the hill to a parallel contour line, and this put us on the path out. On another day with better light, we discovered that we had been circling a knoll on the mountainside.

After a night's sleep so short you wouldn't have wasted a sleeping pill on it, we started in at first light to retrieve the deer. Finding our way in proved considerably easier than finding our way out. Sunlight has its advantages. But for me, spotting the hanging deer proved more difficult than finding Waldo. I couldn't until my buddy pointed it out. That's because it wore camo.

Suspended in the trees, well out of reach of stray dogs or coyotes, hung a four-point buck wearing my buddy's knee-length camo raincoat with the hood up. Two forked prongs stuck out of the hood, visible along with its black nose.

Looking at his sheepish expression, I again asked the obvious.

"Why is the deer wearing your raincoat?"

His answer was simply, "It was raining. I didn't want him to get wet."

In some world, that made sense. But here, having walked out in hypothermia weather, meandering lost in the fog while your deer wore your raincoat, it struck me as odd. But then I realized the cold hard truth.

Hemingway would have approved.

Custer's Last
Deer Stand

If someone named a deer-stand company after me, it would be called Custer's Last Deer Stand. He was famous for his downfall; I'm famous for mine.

My history with deer stands began back when two boards in the crook of a tree was considered elaborate. From there, I graduated to a collapsible climbing stand, which seemed well named. Mine collapsed.

Falling from trees is now something that I've become adept at. Part of the problem, no doubt, is the gravity of the situation. In other words, what goes up must come down, but unfortunately, not at the time of my choosing.

Perhaps a contributing factor is that I always carry too much gear. While I'm climbing, I'm never sure if I'm going up or pulling the tree down. Not that I carry it all on my back. I attach much of it to a rope, which makes me feel like I'm climbing with an anchor.

Then, as soon as I get comfortable, something falls out. Occasionally, it's something I can do without like water or a flashlight. But often, I'm dropping arrows or shells. You'd think just by walking up to my tree that I'd surrendered.

To make matters worse, I'm scared of heights. If I only climbed as high as I feel comfortable, I'd stop so low that I could use the ground as a footrest. It would be like hunting from a park bench.

Climbing a tree when you're scared of heights makes as much sense as frog gigging when you're scared of the dark. But I do that, too.

Another part of the difficulty stems from trying to climb without sounding like someone dropped a washing machine through an oak tree. These sorts of noises are likely to spook deer because there's nothing natural about such clatter unless the deer was raised in a laundromat.

Typically, my downfall begins when the stand loses its grip of the tree. You almost have to be a forest ranger to use one of these things. For instance, on a lot of trees the bark peels and gives the stand no traction at all. Maybe trees in hunting areas could be marked with little signs that read "Climb Here" or "For Idiots Only."

Peeling bark also causes frustration to set in. There's something disheartening about spending five minutes climbing twenty feet only to retrace your progress in five seconds.

My stand, for instance, is supposed to ratchet down. My style, however, is less of a ratchet and more of a rocket. At times like this, I've wondered if Ripley's Believe It or Not! has speed records for deer-stand descent.

Besides the frustration, climbing with a tree stand involves some level of pain. Standard gear for a deer stand should include something besides a safety belt. I'm thinking of shin and arm guards at least, maybe even an airbag.

Speaking of safety gear, the safety-harness manuals read like they were designed to either scare you out of climbing or to send you in a rush to buy insurance. Up until I read mine, I didn't realize there were so many ways to fall out of a tree.

By trial and error, I've now developed criteria for the perfect deer-stand tree. To start with, it doesn't even have to be near a deer. I'll settle for one I won't fall out of.

A good tree for climbing is straight, limbless, and surrounded by soft ground. Normally, you'll want to avoid locust trees, unless hugging a cactus is your idea of a good time. Likewise, you'll also want to have a clear idea on the appearance of poison oak.

Climbing isn't my only problem with deer stands. When it comes to tree stands, I'm like a four-year-old dressed to play in the snow. As soon as I get settled, Mother Nature calls. You'd think just once it could be a busy signal or wrong number, but no, it always happens when I'm twenty feet up and twenty miles from the nearest porta john.

Another lesson I've learned is to pay attention as I climb. For example, should you find yourself attached to a tree trunk at eye level with a hornet's nest, you don't have a lot of choices even though the hornets do.

Bugs don't seem to leave me alone at any elevation. I've seen gnat clouds so thick I expected thunder and lightning to come out.

And they know they've got you. You're more captive than the future groom at his fiancée's bridal shower.

The last lesson I should pass on is that deer-stand maintenance is a self-correcting discipline. By that I mean that if you don't drop everything to do it, you'll eventually drop everything when you don't.

Perhaps what chaps me most is that these things aren't even that comfortable. With all I've learned about tree stands, maybe I should start my own company, even form a partnership and have them made by La-Z-Boy.

When they hit the market, you'll have no trouble figuring out which one is mine. They'll be advertised as Custer's Last Deer Stand.

Pondering
Deer Stuff

Given the importance of accuracy to hunters, I should begin by clarifying my position toward pondering deer stuff. What I do is ponder stuff about deer, not actual deer stuff.

Accuracy seems to me the real issue in pondering, sitting as I do for hours on end in a deer stand, spending so much of my time not actually shooting deer. For a bunch who invests so much time and money to be accurate, hunters aren't very when it comes to deer hunting.

For instance, why do we call it a stand if we sit? I rarely see anyone stand on their stands and never hear anyone refer to their deer seat.

While we're on stands, it occurred to me that although self-climbing portable stands are portable, they are not self-climbing. I'm the one doing the climbing, not them.

In fact, I could see some real problems with self-climbing stands. What if it takes off without you? How would you ever get up there and get it back? Do these things have a safety on them somewhere that I haven't found yet? Of course, I might pay extra for one that was self-climbing, even if I needed a backup stand to go get it.

As you can see, I spend a lot of time pondering these things. But that's just the beginning.

I'm still trying to figure out why we call it deer hunting. This implies that I'm out searching for them. What I do is more like *deer waiting*.

The closest I come to hunting is when I scout, which again, makes little sense since I use no scouts in the process. There may be a merit badge for this, and I could be depriving them of the opportunity. I should probably check it out.

The other thing that makes no sense about scouting is that we spend three days to find a spot two miles from the road in the roughest terrain we can find in hopes of shooting a two-hundred-pound deer, knowing we then have to drag it out. Think about it. The deer wasn't here to begin with, or we'd have scared it away. It came from somewhere else, probably a flat spot near the truck. So why don't we instead scout for this somewhere-else spot that's not so much work? Maybe if I used real scouts, then I could find it.

Another area I ponder is the deer's senses. Take their sight, for example; they're color-blind. We know this. So why don't we buy camo in some colors other than green, brown, and black? The deer don't care. How about red, pink, yellow, and international orange, maybe all on one shirt? Come to think of it, I've got some old leisure suits from my disco days that might work just fine.

Hearing is another good sense to think about. Take rattling. I'm not sure I understand this yet. Here I am, sitting way up in a stand, not standing, mind you, but sitting, rattling two antlers together to attract a buck. Don't you think it could seem just a tad fishy that another buck might be thirty feet off the ground banging his antlers? Maybe bucks aren't responding because they're territorial. Maybe they're coming in to see how that other deer got thirty feet up in a tree. Perhaps they wonder if he jumped a ride on a self-climbing stand.

And this whole sense of smell has got me really stumped. The concoctions that we sprinkle on our clothes and around the stands where we sit quite frankly stink. Does anyone truly believe that a good whiff of this stuff is a pleasant experience for deer? I know if it was people stuff, I wouldn't. So maybe the reason deer respond is that they're mad and want to see who is sprinkling this stuff all over their woods.

Some manufacturers tout their scents as being the strongest on the market, like that's a good thing. It makes you wonder if deer can hold their breath.

The makers of these scents may be catching on, however, since now they're also making cover scents that smell like nothing. What should we call these? Nonsense?

While we're on scents, it amazes me that hunters spend so much effort on deer lure and then carry their lunches into the stands where they sit. Does it really make sense to eat a ham sandwich in the woods? Do you think a deer might get a clue when it figures out what happened to that pig?

And what about jerky? All hunters eat jerky. Has anyone ever actually jerked jerky? A slight yank, a little tug, but jerk? What is that? The motion your hand makes when flying away from your mouth when you finally tear off part of a strip? Don't you wonder if any hunter ever flung his dentures off through the woods attached to a difficult piece of jerky?

And wouldn't it be scary if he nodded off and woke up to find that a chipmunk had wedged those choppers into his mouth and climbed up on a stump beside him with a big grin and a piece of jerky stuck in his teeth?

As you see, pondering can take some bizarre turns.

Like this, for example. It's widely known that most hunting-accident victims are shot by people they know. If that's the case, why don't more of us hunt with strangers?

Lastly, when we're lucky enough to shoot a deer, why do we call it cleaning when we make such a mess? Or dressing when we're taking the hide off?

I've reached two conclusions from all this pondering. First, for a bunch that depends so much on accuracy, we're not, you know. And second, looking over the thoughts that go through my head when I ponder, I may be getting up just a little too early.

A Class in Ethics

Forestry students at Virginia Tech have to learn about more than trees, and a few decades back, I found myself in the fall quarter taking physics and calculus. They were curriculum requirements forestry students viewed like castor oil. You pinched your nose and got them over with. English was not either professor's first language, so I also should have been given foreign language credits.

At that time, I was testing a different approach to studying. Instead of cramming all night on the rush of Morning Thunder tea, I did the heavy work two days before and relaxed the night before the test. Just being rested, I told myself, had to help me think. So when I got an invitation to bowhunt whitetails the afternoon before my physics and calculus midterms, it seemed like the perfect way to prepare for these exams. Maybe being relaxed did help me think, just not prioritize.

My state-of-the-art archery gear consisted of a Fred Bear recurve bow, fiberglass-shafted broadheads with razor inserts, and a three-fingered leather shooting glove. All of this was special ordered through the local hardware store and delivered on the truck along with mattocks and tenpenny nails. The broadheads arrived so dull I had to file them to have a decent edge. I wore red, yellow, and orange camo, having heard that deer were color-blind, and hunters usually weren't. I referred to it as my clown suit.

The farm we hunted was thirty minutes from school in the Blue Ridge Mountains. A ridge ran behind the house and crossing it led to extensive patches of hardwoods and small pastures. In front of the ridge, the farmer kept a hayfield cut close with two apple trees in it. The apples had begun to fall, and the deer left signs of frequent visits. My guess was that they visited mostly at night.

Our plan was to hunt the last few hours until dark. Mike, who had no exams and thought this trip a great idea, crossed the ridge and used a portable stand to get above a trail we had found earlier. I decided that if the deer were hitting the apples after dark, they might be staging in the hardwoods late in the afternoon to be first in line. So I set up twenty yards inside the woods in a ground blind thrown together with fallen branches and loose debris.

The leaves were mostly off the oaks, maples, and hickories carpeting the ground in colors matching my clown suit. I watched clouds rolling in from the north and felt a light breeze that stirred the ground foliage where it grew thickest near the edge of the woods.

When the four-pointer came into view, I first saw his head and fork horns above this foliage. His head would drop down to feed then spring back up when either a branch moved or an acorn fell. He seemed alert but not spooked. At sixty yards, he was beyond my comfort zone for a good shot. But I still had some daylight.

He kept angling my way, dropping his head to feed, popping back up for a look, and then taking a few steps. The path he took paralleled the field but was deeper into the woods than I had set up. When he reached the point that I guessed would be his closest to me, I estimated a thirty-five-yard shot. Drawing while his head was down, I took aim and released.

Just as his head came up my arrow hit a limb and shattered in midair. The half with the point stuck in the ground beneath the deer. The largest piece with the fletching sailed over his back and landed about ten feet past him.

The next part surprised me. Since the arrow mostly landed beyond him, the buck took a few steps toward me while looking away. My next shot found its way through the branches and hit just behind his shoulder. The deer bolted and I sat there shaking like a kid on a twenty-five-cent amusement pony.

I gave the buck thirty minutes to lie down and found Mike. We went back to my blind, picked up the blood trail, and a couple hundred yards later found a pool of blood. In the dark we kept losing the trail, circling back like hounds before striking out in another direction. Just before midnight, no closer despite hours of searching, we decided to come back at sunrise.

That left me with two other problems: physics and calculus. Both midterms counted 40 percent of my grade, so zeros on them would flunk me out of each class. The knot in my stomach tightened on the drive home. I hardly slept, but by sunrise knew what I had to do.

I wrote notes to each professor, went to their offices, and slipped under each of their doors an explanation that I had to miss their exams for personal reasons and that I would like to make them up upon my return. Then I drove back to the woods with Mike. On the way, a steady rain began to fall. With each drop, our odds of finding the deer slowly melted.

We went to the last place we had found blood the night before. It was dissolving and the leaves were flattening, so even tracks were hard to see. We followed each trail as it broke off, and about noon, we found one spoonful of blood mixed with rain in a curled leaf. We never saw another sign.

All afternoon, we walked the woods looking for the buck. We'd heard that deer head to water when hit, so we walked both sides of the creek. We searched all the rhododendron thickets and walked ever-widening circles from the last sign of blood.

As rain, darkness, and hope fell, we finally admitted we were going to lose this one. It's the worst feeling, taking a life in a way that only amounts to loss. No excuses make up for it, not rain, darkness, or exams. We drove back to the school soaked, tired, and hungry. I felt like I was the one gutshot.

The next morning, I made the rounds to catch my professors. My calculus professor sat me down with the exam the minute I walked in. I did fine and went to the physics hall. This one was different.

My physics professor hemmed and hawed, debated with himself in Chinese, and finally decided I could take an exam but not the same one. He told me to come back the next day.

I had a bad feeling that he was going to load for bear and make me pay. So I turned to the physics chapter and went to the back where all the hardest problems were. I worked on them until every one of them was perfect, each step, each calculation, and each formula. Throwing relaxation to the wind, I drank Morning Thunder tea until I could have marked a twenty-acre territory.

Upon my return the next day, my professor met me with one sheet of paper and a smile. I was in an empty classroom, alone except for him watching. Four problems were on the paper. Four hard problems. Four hard problems from the back of my physics book that I had worked to perfection the night before. I still remembered every formula and answer. I made a perfect score and an enemy. He grimaced and wondered if I could have cheated. Had he not stayed to watch, that probably would have been his conclusion.

I'd like for the moral of this story to be that when you do the right thing it all works out. But ethics are messy. We never found the buck I shot and that lost deer still leaves me with a sour taste. My physics professor was so enraged by my perfect midterm that he gave an excruciating final exam and then docked me an additional letter grade for attitude. I passed but paid a price.

Still, as I think about it forty years later, the lessons I learned from those decisions have been more useful than calculus or physics. Little did I know at the time, but we are always enrolled in ethics class.

In Pursuit of Bearded Birds

When there's a turkey on
both ends of the gun.

Bob White, *Long Beard,* pencil on archival paper

How to Name
Your Turkey

The great tales of turkey lore share a common trait, namely that the birds are memorable. The chase, the shot, and the escape all played a role, but somehow, you remember the bird not only for his exploits but also for his moniker. Let's face it; a turkey without a name is like an ant without a picnic.

We should never underestimate the importance of a good turkey tale. Consider this. The weeks of the year that are not turkey season far outnumber the weeks that are turkey season and seem longer yet. Passing all that time will drain most hunters of their stories unless the tales happen to be good enough to be repeated. And what better way to kick off such a story as someone saying, "Tell us that story about Ol' Knotted Beard."

Naming a turkey well is no simple feat. Like the hunt, it takes planning, cunning, and just a little bit of pulling someone's leg. So here are a few principles for naming your turkey.

Let's start with the ones that got away, since in my case, there are more of these. Gobblers that get away deserve more than a one-gun salute; they deserve to become legends. Think of the James Gang, Bonnie and Clyde, or Elmer Fudd's wabbit. If they were captured on their first encounter, no one would remember them. It's the act of repeated escape that made them legends and their names should reflect this.

Good names should make these birds larger than Moby Dick, more tenacious than a snake on a rat, and sharper than Einstein's pencil. Remember, these are birds that would have gotten away from the best hunters, and even more so people like me. Here are some examples.

The Ghost is a name that leaves the impression of being able to disappear at will. He glides through the forest like a fog. The "Swamp Fox" implies a similar trait, plus smarts. This gobbler knows his terrain and how to use it. "Four-Eyed Earl" would be that gobbler no one could sneak up on. Either that or he wears glasses and all his friends cruelly tease him, but it was probably the first one.

Stealth and brains are not the only traits that define a gobbler either. "Ol' Lead Bottom" and "Flak-Jacket Jack" can take a shot and keep on going. Obviously, these names sound better than some that implied you missed.

Naming the gobblers you bagged requires special skill, since your hunting buddies generally get sick of hearing about these, especially if they finished the season empty-handed. A catchy name becomes critical. In this case, the ideal name is one you can drop to make a newcomer ask for the story, particularly in front of your hunting buddies. It could go like this.

Amid discussions about elusive gobblers, you drop in the following introduction. "Well, that bird sounds like Ol' Double-Back Dan . . ." you say, trailing off at the end to imply this story must be dragged out of you.

At this point, the newcomer will be unable to resist and ask, "Who was Double-Back Dan?"

As you begin the story, you might also hear the regulars exclaim as they leave, "I think I left the stove on. I'm late for my kid's recital. Uh, I think I need to hang wallpaper."

Of course, you should ignore the stampede of hunting buddies, try not to choke on the dust cloud they create leaving, and proceed with your story. You might also slyly handcuff the newcomer to his chair as you begin with, "It all started eleven years ago when Double-Back Dan was a poult . . ."

Other names that work equally well include "Pothole Pete," "Dogleg Jake," "Skunked Once Wally," and "Donald Didn't Duck."

You may think naming turkeys is something that happens after they escape or become Thanksgiving dinner. Actually, nothing could be further from the truth. A good name takes planning, the sort you do in a truck, in a blind, or in the bathroom. A proper name makes you look forward to next season, just so you can use it. Here are a few I'm working on while I ponder things.

"Fat Fred" has a nice ring to it and certainly a tone of familiarity. Also, he's obviously a big 'un. "Cowboy Bob" would make a good name for a bird with exceptional spurs. I haven't found him yet. "Methuselah" is a name I'm saving for an old tom, though I don't think they get that old. Likewise, "Rip Van Winkle" hints at age and excessive time on the roost.

Before you start thinking there's nothing to this turkey naming, think again. You also need to be careful to exclude some names.

For instance, never give a gobbler a name that gives away his location, especially if he's still up there. I would resist using "Buzzard Roost Bill," "Shooting Creek Sam," or "Ol' Up-The-Road-A-Mile-Take-A-Left-Drive-To-The-Dead-Oak-Park-And-Walk-Straight-Up-The-Hill Gus."

Likewise, you want to avoid turkey names that imply some lack of skill on your part. This is a role best left to your hunting buddies, who guard this territory like Dobermans and relish needling you more than piranhas dream of meatballs. Examples of names to avoid because they make your turkey sound easy include "Tone-Deaf Toney," "One-Eyed Pete," and, in the event you double, "Dumb and Dumber."

All things considered, few skills in turkey hunting are so neglected and yet so important as creative naming. Practice yelping all you want, pattern your shotgun until you run out of targets, and scout until your Vibrams wear slick, and you may get your bird. But that only helps during the season. If you can't rub it in for the rest of the year, what have you really accomplished?

Now, if you'll excuse me, I have to polish up a few details on the story of a hen I shot this fall. This may sound like no great feat, but you haven't heard "The Tale of the Bearded Lady."

The Turkey
Chainsaw
Massacre

As you wait for the first hint of morning light, few sounds have such a soothing effect as the crickets' soft chirping. That is, soothing until you realize that cricket sound is the same one you heard in *Psycho* right before some nutcase jumped into the shower with a butcher knife. On occasion, turkey hunts can take on the nature of a cheap horror film. Mine could have been titled "The Turkey Chainsaw Massacre."

Like any scary flick, this hunt began normally. The weather was mild, the night sky full of stars, and except for an occasional rooster's crow, the only other sound was that eerie bunch of crickets.

Shortly after dawn, a lone crow drifted across the sky, calling in a raspy voice as if possessed. Others of his kin answered, haunting the forest like a gathering of evil spirits. They landed in the tops of the oaks like spies of some dark force.

A cloud of pollen danced in the first beams of the sun. This golden cloud drifted like a pretty poison, perhaps poppy dust dropped by the Wicked Witch of the West from *The Wizard of Oz*. I glanced upward, hoping to see a swarm of flying monkeys, and wondered if they were in season and good to eat. I could have gone for a mess of monkey about now.

Even if they had come, I'd obviously brought the wrong decoys. But it was just pollen and there were no flying monkeys. Still, it filled our sinuses and watered our eyes. Camo hoods offer no defense from such an attack. I fought back a sneeze. My son blinked to erase this golden grit from his pupils.

As the crows commenced to call again, one lone warrior answered defiantly, a fat old gobbler who claimed these woods.

"What was that?" asked my son.

I looked at him with disbelief. This gargling warbler—the turkey, not the son—sounded like a water hose full of gravel. Maybe the old bird suffered as much from pollen as we did.

I whispered back, "That, my boy, is what we're here for."

I returned his call with an inviting yelp, deceptive and seductive. I pretended to flirt as best I could with this overweight Thanksgiving dinner.

The crows reacted to our conversation. They began to swarm, milling about as if to remind me this was their horror film. I expected to see the ground disgorging centipedes and other foul creatures of Middle Earth, but my eyes watered from the pollen and whenever I looked down my hood slid forward, and I couldn't see a cotton-picking thing. For all I knew, I was being eaten by ants and lizards. Then he gobbled again.

The hairs on my neck rose up. His garbled, throaty blathering came from a much closer point. He'd been sneaking as I'd been contemplating creepy crawlers. The sun had crested the treetops, lime green with new growth. All this was promising, except for the ominous murder of crows milling about somewhere over this noble bird.

I hit the slate a couple more times and hoped he'd catch sight of my decoys, mistake my hen for his best girl, and realize she was being courted by some young whippersnapper of a jake, even if he was made of molded plastic.

He gobbled again and my blood ran cold.

We went on like this for what was probably minutes but seemed like hours. The gobbler got to be old for a reason, and I'd been skunked so far this season for the same reason. He was smarter than me. Still, I knew I had something on my side—dumb luck. This reassured me until I realized that dumb luck isn't the same as good luck.

In an instant, the crows cranked up to a new level, took wing and left. I wondered what dreaded visitor could drive off such a horrendous gathering of birds. The gobbler fell quiet. Only the crickets seemed louder and louder and louder until I looked over my shoulder expecting to see the glint of a butcher knife.

Instead, I heard a deafening roar that nearly made me jump from my camo and streak through the woods in my Fruit of the Looms screaming like a schoolgirl chased by boys with toads.

Waaaaaaah, wah, wah, waaaaaaaah, roared this horror that I knew had wreaked havoc on my turkey hunt. The chainsaw screamed from only fifty yards away and soon was echoed by another. An entire pulpwood crew assaulted the silence, and I knew that one wise old gobbler was about to disappear into the deep woods like a vampire at daybreak.

I guessed about where he would cross the fence that marked the boundary line and made a mad dash for it, son in tow. We got there just in time to watch this majestic but overweight flying fat boy flap as best he could through a pine thicket.

We sat and caught our breath. No hero came to our rescue. No wizard offered a magic potion for our use. No bluebird landed on my shoulder to whisper wisdom in my ear.

We'd just survived what one shot could have turned into the Turkey Chainsaw Massacre. But that shot was never fired. No massacre occurred.

Still, it might have if I could have gotten my hands around the neck of that pulpwood cutter.

Almost a Lion Story

I had just sat down to pen a story about a man-eating lion stalking a hunter through darkest Africa. The hunter was in turn tracking a wounded water buffalo and the dense vegetation was going to bring all three into close contact at the watering hole. Clearly, death lurked in the tall grass. Then my phone chirped.

Phones don't ring anymore; rather than having to race into the kitchen to grab it before it stops ringing, you can now look at the number and decide whether you want to talk. It was a turkey-hunting buddy named JC, so I took the call.

JC then proceeded to tell me about his hunt. He began with the details about waking before sunrise, stopping at the Waffle House, and flirting with the waitress who called him Sugar. I assured him she calls everyone Sugar and to just focus on the turkey hunt.

He went on to describe how he had scouted, used locator calls, set up his decoy, and waited for sunrise. Apparently, the deer were all over him since they were out of season.

Then another hunter stalked his decoy and he had to wave him off. He asked if shooting hen decoys when hens were out of season was illegal and I told him that I didn't think so. Stupidity is rarely illegal. At least, not often enough.

Then, during a lull in the action, he sensed something unusual and realized he had picked up a tick. This tick had lodged in an unlikely spot north of some extremities and south of others, if you get my drift. How it navigated the layers and repellant made me think it would have done well as a man-eating lion in the jungles of darkest Africa stalking a hunter. Perhaps better, since this tick caught one.

After that, JC apparently took a lunch break, set up his stand on another site, and waited until the turkeys went to roost. Having put in a full day, he now felt obligated to call me up and let me know how it went.

Although the details were interesting, JC could have just as easily summed it up as follows:

"Hey Jim," JC would say.

"Yep?"

"Went turkey hunting today."

"Get anything?"

"Nope."

"OK, see ya."

"You too."

Had he condensed his day and shortened his call, I might not have been so distracted and could have finished that story about the man-eating lion. I always hate to leave a hunter, a man-eating lion, and a wounded water buffalo in the jungle while death lurks.

In any event, this was almost a lion story.

Growing
Your Gobbler

Gobblers grow to trophy size in two different ways. First, smart old gobblers grow long in the beak by dodging turkey hunters. They simply outsmart us until old age sets in. This allows them to develop long beards and extra weight, sort of like us. Second, gobblers have a habit of growing for several years after they are tagged. Wildlife biologists have a term for this latter phenomenon; they call it lying.

Amongst turkey hunters, we call it "the best I can recollect." Precise details only tend to muck up a good story for most of us. The trick to getting away with a bit of elaboration, however, is to use colorful language.

By this, I do not mean you should lie about statistics, such as weights or the lengths of their beards. Remember, you might have had witnesses. Instead, I'm suggesting you paint a picture. After all, if a picture is worth a thousand words, the reverse must also be true.

Below are examples of elongations of the truth, or as I like to call them, Great Gobbler Growers. To test your abilities at gobbler growing, simply review this list and decide whether any of these might apply to your bird. Check off each one that does.

GREAT GOBBLER GROWERS

1) He was a heavy bird. Weight Watchers wanted him for a mascot.
2) One reason I was able to bag him is that he kept tripping on his beard.
3) I don't remember his exact size, but he was big. I saw two hens using him for shade.
4) Spurs? His were so long they were illegal weapons in seventeen states.
5) When I got him home and showed him to the kids, they cried. They thought I had shot Big Bird.

6) He was an intimidating gobbler. When he showed up, my decoy ran away.
7) Something I might have forgotten to mention was that when I found his roost, the tree was leaning.
8) Talk about a heavy bird, he wore knee braces.
9) The hens weren't following him; they were in orbit.
10) When the game biologists put him on a scale the Surgeon General issued a warning.
11) He didn't just have his own territory; he had his own zip code.
12) No joke. They put him on the Wheaties box.
13) He was so big he didn't wait for acorns to drop; he picked them.
14) Talk about a heavy bird. He beeped when he backed up.
15) For this bird to fly off the roost, he had to get clearance from air traffic control.
16) A big fan? It had a three-horsepower motor.
17) When he gobbled, it measured a seven on the Richter scale.
18) They made a movie about him when he was a young gobbler. You might have heard of it. It was called *Big Jake*.
19) His wingspan was really impressive. At the check-in station they put his species down as Boeing 747.
20) When I tagged him, I had to use a license plate.

Now, look back over the list and count your check marks. If you counted fifteen to twenty that described your bird, consider yourself lucky you're not Pinocchio or your nose could crack your truck windshield. Clearly, though, you do tell an elaborate yarn.

If you checked ten to fourteen, you probably do have a trophy or two tucked away. Of course, by now it sounds like a dozen or so.

Should your score fall in the five to nine range, you could use a little polishing up on your truth stretching. For practice, you might try hanging out with fishermen.

Finally, if you checked off less than five of these, you're either overly humble or much too honest. These are unusual traits when it comes to reporting on our trophies. But then again, there is one other possibility. Maybe you've been mistaken all this time and you've been shooting quail.

Of Ducks and Dogs

Cold mornings can make
your brain freeze.

Bob White, *A School of Thought—Drake Wood Duck,* pencil on archival paper

Blurred
Memories

Ducks fly through my memories. The set wings of a mallard with dangling orange feet have become a blended image of all the mallards taunting me over the years. Places fade. Directions not written have erased. Still, one season remains crisp in my mind for its novelty, newness, and absurdity.

A mountain kid studying at Virginia Tech, I was introduced to a new professor who grew up in South Louisiana and wanted to find some ducks. We quickly reached an agreement with me providing the "where" if he'd provide the "how." Somewhere in the fine print was a clause I missed on how much stuff I'd help carry but be well fed for it.

The cast of characters included Fontenot, nicknamed after listening to his Justin Wilson albums, Fontenot's wife, and Duke. Two things you should know about the wife and the dog. First, she was also Cajun and whatever made it to the game pot was smothered in Cajun seasonings in a deceptive brown roux and served over rice. The first bite I took of smothered game singed my hair from the inside and not one particle has fallen out since. She might have become rich with this preventive for baldness had we known it sooner.

Second, Duke came from South Louisiana as well and had a personality like his owner. Sure, the pup was sleek and strong, but he hunted hard and played harder. On the drive to the duck blind he'd lie in the back seat of the old Dodge crunching aluminum beer cans until they were gone. Maybe he passed them, but I don't remember ever seeing the shrapnel.

Once that season, I stayed over to avoid an early drive after a late night, sleeping in the basement with Duke who charged me one boot for the privilege. He gave me a partial refund in the morning, if you count the sole and strings as change. On another night before a hunt, Duke found a case of liquor in the basement, removed only the sherry, four bottles out of a dozen others, and chewed the tops off and lapped up the contents. A hungover Lab is a still partner in a duck blind.

Virginia's duck season kicked off in the early fall with a few days to wave off gnats while you throw your barrel at racing wood ducks. We hunted the New River in stretches flat enough to wade, but wide enough the woodies could easily avoid us. Still, we did our homework, made some good guesses on flight plans, and dropped our first ducks of the season. I replenished my fly-tying supplies with a few years' worth of flank feathers and smothered duck made me look forward to the main season.

Opening day for the November season was like one-card draw from a poker deck. You had fifty-two choices for weather, and we drew hard rain. The river rose too high to hunt the islands we'd used in wood duck season and the mallards needed slower water to sit in.

We found a bend where the water backed up and the decoys would just about hold. Ours were weighted with railroad spikes that we picked up walking the tracks to and from the blind. They held the decoys well but carried like a sack of rocks. Where the river washed up, the bank lay up against a stand of oaks. Brush from older floods piled up into a natural blind, so all we had to do was set decoys in high water in the dark. The usual duck-hunting stuff.

At first light, Fontenot quacked a few times and mallards started dropping through the trees. Not out where we could shoot mind you, but back behind us on wet ground. Puddles full of acorns may have drawn them in. But we quickly began to stalk and jump shoot mallards in the woods.

Every flushed mallard caught us by surprise. They came up beside us, at our feet, and behind us in places where no duck should have flushed. Duke found what we hit, but after walking through flooded timber with ducks flushing like sprung mousetraps, our nerves were wound tight as the spring on a cheap watch.

Having walked the woods, we circled back up the river's edge to our blind. I blame the next part on our flooded ducks, but one of our decoys had worked downstream in the rising current and the railroad spike had snagged on an underwater tree root. Whenever a surge of water or debris pulled the cord, the decoy tipped up like a feeding duck. Fontenot saw it and began to stalk.

I recognized what had happened before Fontenot did since this was one of my decoys, but quickly decided a sacrificed decoy would be a small price to pay for a tale of Fontenot taking ducks on the water. I watched as his gun rose, my sides already quivering from suppressed laughter, and when the duck tipped one last time, his safety clicked off. When the decoy bobbed back up, I figured it a goner. But in that split second, Fontenot realized something was wrong with a mallard that didn't flush, or he just made a sporting decision. Hearing my snickering, he grabbed the decoy, mumbled some Cajun insults my way, and we laughed all the way back to the blind.

The cold came in December that season. To the east, the Chesapeake Bay froze solid, and first responders ran food to the islanders by helicopter. The New River was colder yet. The water froze in sheets that would break off in the current and floes of ice floated down and piled up on rocks, sometimes on edge, with jagged horizons replacing rounded boulders.

To the north, the New River dumps into the Ohio River, so our best hunting usually came when it was cold someplace else, like Ohio. The freeze turned the ducks south in variety and numbers. Black ducks drew us into single-digit weather, where our shivering forms were no more than dark huddling shapes in sleet that always found the crease between your cap and collar, rolling like pins and needles when it found bare skin. On one of these mornings, Fontenot was teaching, so I went ahead and set the decoys. His plan was to follow after class.

Sitting on a bucket in an ice-glazed blind, I remember the sun rose brilliantly but without heat. Fog rolled in wisps down the river like Lee's army retreating. Except for the crows, nothing living moved. The water gurgled, the ice groaned, an occasional limb snapped like it had finally given up. I remained motionless until Fontenot arrived.

His first question was something like, "Seen any ducks?" and my answer was something like, "Grrfntly." My ability to speak had evaporated with my body heat, and I learned of an early sign of hypothermia. Stomping in a sunny spot and drinking hot liquids was enough to get me back in the hunt, but it was a useful lesson. To this day, I talk to myself if for no other reason than to check my physical state. Of course, it leaves a poor impression of my mental state.

The cold up north continued to push nonresident ducks our way. One morning, I was teased by a flock of over forty pintails, circling too high to shoot, dipping for a closer inspection of my decoy set, and whistling every time they flared.

But it was big ducks that drew us out during the holidays, the mallards and the black ducks, toughened by their trip south. We swore they were Canadians and bigger and tougher. But they ate well, and the Cajun spices were beginning to insulate my blood like antifreeze.

At season's end, the cold broke with a warm rain that brought the New River to its highest point of the season. All the ice floes melted, and the runoff turned riffles into rapids. Only fools would hunt the last day and Fontenot convinced me to go.

We loaded the gear and Lab into his pirogue, strapped on life jackets, and began to wade and swim to our favorite island. With one of us hanging on each end, the pirogue carried us through the holes and eventually our feet found rocks. When we reached the island, the water was too strong for our decoy weights to hold, so we were constantly going to the lower end of the island to retrieve and reset them at the upper end.

Sometime in the afternoon, a sole mallard flared over the decoys and Fontenot dropped him. Duke retrieved and the season ended. We began to pick up decoys and Duke dragged in his share as was his custom. The only time he ever brought in a decoy was when we did. He piled them on the bank like it was part of his job.

In the fading light, we had to push the pirogue back to the bank, up and across current, and the going was slow. We approached the bank well past shooting time. In the darkness, a flashlight flickered.

Funny how if you hunt with another fellow enough, you learn to recognize his flashlight. Maybe by its dimness or a red band of plastic that glows around the bulb, but we knew this was a hunting buddy who saw our car and stopped to check on us well after normal quitting time.

In typical what-the-hell fashion, Fontenot greets him by shouting, "There's the game warden . . . let's shoot him!"

At this point, a considerably brighter beam came on that was obviously government issue. It drew us to the bank like a *Star Trek* tractor beam. As it turns out, our buddy was not so much concerned about our well-being as our running into the game warden unannounced. After all, one of us had almost shot a decoy on the water earlier in the season.

Our season ended with a grumpy game warden going through all our decoys, sacks, licenses, and pirogue looking for a violation to write us up on. He checked our magazines, inspected every shell, and counted our duck three times. Then he mumbled like he had hypothermia and left.

Seasons since struggle to compare. Ducks have jumped in front of me from Rocky Mountain beaver ponds and streaked by Chesapeake Bay blinds, occasionally falling. Retrievers have broken ice on valiant retrieves and worked against tides to drop ducks at my feet with a grin and their tongues hanging.

But all the memories blur together like graying black-and-white Polaroids in a photo album, save for one season with a Cajun duck hunter, a dog who defined retrievers for me, and a Cajun lady who introduced me to smothered duck. So, when the wind blows and my joints creak, I'll pour a brandy and remember the one season that stands crisp in my memory and ask forgiveness of a game warden who thought we threatened to shoot him.

A Quack's Guide
to Duck Calls

The essential duck calls—everything from the basic quack to pintail whistling—have been covered more thoroughly than grandma's knees. In fact, if these were the most essential calls to know, we wouldn't need additional instruction on the topic. For the average duck hunter, though, like me, the more critical calls have been largely ignored. To be blunt, the most important calls aren't even made to ducks. Allow me to elaborate.

Feeder Chuckle. Duck season seems to last only a few weeks and the period preparing for and recovering from duck hunting can go on forever. That's why the most common activities of duck hunters are eating and telling tall tales. When these occur simultaneously, you will experience what is referred to as the Feeder Chuckle.

Imagine for instance that Brad is telling for the fortieth time the story about taking his boss duck hunting. During this trip, the boss gets the patched waders, the patches blow in waist-deep water, the boss panics in the rush of ice water to his straddle, he grabs Brad by the collar, and the two proceed to commune with fishes. Even though you've heard this story every time it was ever told, you forget how long the lead is and you load your mouth with mashed potatoes just as Brad hits the punch line. Caught in the moment, you must laugh out loud without blowing potatoes. This skill is commonly referred to as the Feeder Chuckle.

Mastering the Feeder Chuckle takes skill and practice. During the off-season, you can train by gorging yourself with peanut butter and watching *Seinfeld* reruns or listening to *A Prairie Home Companion* while gulping down a strawberry milkshake. Perhaps the best simulation, however, is stuffing your cheeks with popcorn and listening to tapes of Jerry Clower or Justin Wilson.

Highball. This call is often referred to as the *hail call* and is typically practiced in places named something like The Dew Drop Inn. Late at night, this call is typically slurred.

Even though this is not a complicated call to perform, you can practice it too much.

Lonesome Hen. This call often follows excessive use of the Highball, especially when hunting far from home. Let me offer two words for the married guys here: steel shot. In other words, if you don't steel yourself against this call, you might get shot.

Comeback Call. I use this one a lot. It can be effective, but this varies with the depth of the water, the consistency of the mud, and the impenetrable nature of the surrounding vegetation. An example may shed some light on the delicate tones of this call.

The last time I used it was just as I finished setting my spread, about thirty minutes before sunrise. Chip, my Lab, had disappeared. Ducks could be heard sailing overhead on whistling wings and an occasional splash made out as they landed.

The challenge was to call Chip in without scaring the ducks. It went like this.

"Chip, come." Harsh whisper.

No splashing dog noises.

"Chip," pause, "Come!" Harsher whisper.

The silence shattered with Chip's barking about one hundred yards up in the woods. Clearly, he'd jumped a rabbit. No amount of Comeback Calls was likely to work, but at this moment, reason could not prevail.

Abandoning the whisper, I yelled, "Chip, get your sorry lard butt back here now!"

At this moment, the hunt deteriorated dramatically due to my overuse of the Comeback Call. Ducks flushed all around me in the darkness. The best option I had left was to take up rabbit hunting.

Pleading Call. This one is usually made after the hunt is over. Picture this. You're home five hours late, even the back door is bolted, no lights are on, and you can't get in. You're hoarse from excessive Comeback Calls, you're suffering from overuse of the Highball, you stained your hunting shirt while muffing a Feeder Chuckle, and, truth be told, you have a lingering hint of perfume from a Lonesome Hen.

Now you must exercise the most important skill—opening the back door at two a.m. with a Pleading Call. It usually goes like this:

"But Honey, Brad was driving."

"Chip was lost in the swamp. You know you like Chip."

"Honest, this smell is kerosene and the Lonesome Hen belonged to Brad. You know how single guys are."

All the other calls are useless if you never master this one.

In summary, remember these universal calling tips.

First, you can call too much, especially with the Highball.

Second, if you get the right response on the first call, shut up.

Third, always use a call that works with the species you're calling to. For instance, Chip probably has no idea what "lard butt" even means.

Fourth, not all calls work all the time. In other words, sometimes you just have to go get the dog.

Finally, hunter safety begins at home. That's just one more reason to take it easy on the Highball and avoid the Lonesome Hen. Under these circumstances, no hunter has completely perfected the Pleading Call.

Reasons for Owning a Dog

I was talking to myself the other day when an argument broke out. It didn't turn into fisticuffs or anything, but that was when I realized I needed a dog.

Dogs have many character traits that people should imitate. For instance, if I had a dog when I started arguing with myself, I likely would have been talking to my dog instead. He probably would have agreed with me and diffused the argument before it escalated.

Had anyone been passing by, they would have thought I was talking to my dog, which is perfectly normal, rather than talking to myself, which just makes me look like an old fool.

Then there are always the occasional odd smells that older gentlemen create, which can be blamed on the dog. When you ask the dog about it, he will never deny being the culprit.

Another thing dogs are good at is greeting people. I've never seen one that doesn't get excited when you visit, so much so they often put their hosts to shame. Dogs jump around and wag their tails far more than their owners do.

In general, dogs only have two moods: happy and asleep. Both have their benefits.

If I could copy one habit of dogs it would be their ability to chill. A dog can sleep anytime, curl up anyplace, and be ready to go at the drop of a tailgate. If you have a fire lit, your dog can fall asleep before you can and probably while closer to the fire than you are.

Take a dog camping and he becomes an accessory. Anything starts to roll away? The dog will fetch it. Gathering firewood? The dog can carry at least one stick and may chew it down to kindling by the time you need to light the fire.

Concerned about roving critters? Dogs not only keep an eye on camp, but they also do a nice job discouraging intruders.

Once the night turns cool and it's time for bed, a dog is like an electric blanket. They call them "three dog nights" for a reason. You may just need to be a little assertive to keep them outside the sleeping bag.

Dogs occasionally bark, but even then, it's just a cautionary warning or alert that precedes biting. Sometimes it never elevates beyond a bark and that's the way it should be. In fact, the subject that caused the dog to bark could soon become its best friend and everyone gets along afterwards. The infraction is never logged for future reference.

If it were up to me, every corporate office would have to be staffed with a dog, preferably a Labrador retriever. Larger companies may even need one per department. Their employees could learn a lot from them.

For starters, Labs always get along. They are the ultimate team players. When it's time for a meeting, as soon as everyone gets up to go, the Lab will follow.

If the meeting becomes contentious, the Lab should mediate. He could cast the tie-breaking vote on difficult issues as he would be happy to do so, and no one would hold a grudge for having him do it.

Labs also boost morale. Just imagine yourself having a bad day when eighty pounds of goodwill walks to your desk, tongue hanging out in that goofy Lab smile. For a scratch behind his ears, he does a good job, and you go back to work in a better mood.

You could even put him on the security team. Unless someone broke in and thought to bring doggy treats, he would probably bark and sound the alarm.

Then there's the age-old issue of leftovers in the company fridge. Pass a rule that after two days all food gets Rovered. Solved that one.

All in all, a Lab would be the perfect employee if he could be a bit more careful with the company car.

Besides being good employees, dogs excel in their people skills. Dogs rarely interrupt you in the middle of a story, unless of course they need to go outside. They tend to be excellent listeners and never talk out of school. I've never heard one exaggerate or repeat a story as his own. In general, dogs are honest sorts.

The only exception is when a bird dog false points on quail. Even then, the dog's not lying; he just made a mistake. Some sparrow that probably had been consorting with quail momentarily confused the dog. But he sorts it out soon enough and both of you just move on.

So, I've about talked myself into getting a dog. I'm sure the puppy in him will be contagious and perhaps he can teach me a thing or two.

My Steel Shot Rusted

Since the early days of duck hunting, most of us have been waiting for steel shot. Sure, you'll hear guys talk about the good old days, shooting lead in a ten-gauge shotgun, having it carry for two hundred yards and dropping a duck stone-cold. But admit it. Steel is better, because now you have an excuse.

All of us have missed ducks we should have hit, even with lead shot. Before, we could blame the sun, the fog, the wind, poor visibility from the blind, the dog's disposition, or the bad coffee. Yet all these excuses eventually came back to our skill under adverse conditions, or at least, conditions we could adapt to. We could have moved, sold the dog, waited for it to clear off, clear-cut the blind, bought a new gun, or not brought yesterday's coffee.

But now, there is no solution for steel shot. It's the government's fault. Remember the people who brought us taxes? These are the same people who told us to use steel shot. It's the law and we have no choice. So who gets the blame when I miss a duck?

The government.

When that occasional duck blasts through your spread and shrugs off every pellet you can unload at it, you can explain to any witnesses exactly who is to blame and just what's wrong with steel shot. In case you haven't identified its faults on your own, allow me to share a few of my observations.

For starters, on a rainy day, who will argue when you look out from under a dripping hat brim to exclaim, "I think my steel shot rusted."

Who would have remembered to oil their shells?

And everyone knows that steel is recycled, which is a good thing. It's just odd to think we're shooting with old railroad tracks or junk cars. Maybe we'd have been better off trying to run over the ducks.

Also, everyone knows that steel is drawn to magnets and magnets toward the north pole. Are steel pellets drawn to magnetic north just as ducks are heading south? Maybe my shot's not even going in the right direction.

Hunters are advised to shoot larger pellet sizes when using steel. This means in the same gauge, compared with lead, we have fewer pellets per shell. From my experience, every time I move up in shot size, it gets worse. I might be shooting slugs.

Maybe I've been doing this all wrong. Instead of shooting larger pellets, maybe I should have been hunting smaller ducks.

To make matters worse, the patterns are so tight my gun squeaks. In fact, if the pattern were any tighter, I could shoot a gnat, though I'm not sure it would drop.

This whole thing with steel could just be a matter of density. Not mine, the shot's. I might not be missing; it's just that the pellets are bouncing off.

On the other hand, lead shot is so dense, I might not have been killing ducks as much as I was making them too heavy to fly.

The good thing about steel, though, is that it's lighter; I can carry more shells that way. The bad thing is that I have to.

Let's face it. Steel and lead just shoot differently. For instance, lead pellets deform, and when they do, they fly crooked. After all these years of shooting crooked shells, how can I be expected to hit anything shooting straight?

Steel travels fast, too. You never know if your shot missed the duck or passed it.

Lead also leads differently. You have to consider the range, windage, and the pellets' density and speed. Heck, by the time a fellow can do the math, the duck's gone.

To adjust to all these differences, some hunters just focus on shots at close range. Then, after they miss three times and cuss, they can try using their guns as clubs.

Other hunters just give up on steel and switch to more exotic metals. You practically have to be a metallurgist now just to hunt ducks.

I mean, what exactly is tungsten? Judging from the price of the shells, I'd say it was made from gold.

Finally, you should take special care shooting steel in vintage shotguns. The reason is that old guns can't shoot steel. Apparently, the same goes for old hunters.

Upland Birds

When waving your gun and firing
at least drives away the gnats.

Bob White, *Two in the Hand—Doves,* pencil on archival paper

Hunting the Pole

Doc didn't shoot by the pole this year. To understand, you'd have to know Doc.

Talking to someone on the dove season's opening day every year for nearly twenty years, you learn about them in pieces. It's like putting together a secondhand puzzle that's in the wrong box, so you don't have an image to work from when you start, and the person emerges as the puzzle comes together.

He was cut from an old mold, Doc was. When he smiled, which was often, his whole face changed. Other than the smile, he could have been a sergeant in an old World War II film, short, square-shouldered, with old-timey features like you see in black and white photos from the forties, a guy leaning on the fender of a Buick taking a picture for his best girl. You knew Doc had a best girl.

When I first met Doc, he dove hunted with a little Boykin, hardly more than an inflated bedroom slipper, one of the fuzzy ones. But that little Boykin had Doc's heart. No matter the heat, that Boykin hunted, retrieved, and spit feathers. A floppy-eared bedroom slipper, that was him, and with a dove in his mouth he looked for all the world like he ought to tip over.

One year, I brought my Brittany to fetch birds, and as soon as we released them the two dogs began to circle like cocks. The Brittany figured to show the bedroom slipper who owned the field. The bedroom slipper wanted none of it. After that, we kept the dogs apart.

We hunted a couple years with both dogs in the field, each of us quick to compliment the other as we became better friends. After a while, we joked more, me asking why he didn't get a whole dog, and him wanting to know if I could still find a bird without my Brittany. One day, my Brittany chased a crippled dove across the field, watching it rise slowly off the ground before catching up and taking it right out of the air. Doc wanted to know if I still planned to shoot or just let the dog catch the low-fliers.

On the opening day after Doc's Boykin died, he could hardly tell us without choking up. That dog was like family to him. Surely, it lived in the house, probably watched TV with him. Ate popcorn. A few years later, my Brittany went to sleep the night before opening day and never woke up. Doc knew; that day I hunted without my dog. He knew.

We started coming early to talk, this circle of friends, as the years went by. Larry, at the hub, fixed the fields and coaxed in the birds. An assortment of us came in and out, depending on the field and the year, about five of us always there, telling stories.

Doc would reminisce of trout, wet-wading down mountain streams in a day when people would pick up soggy hitchhikers, muddy from sliding down creek banks, and take them back up the mountain. We'd talk of doubles in a dove field, past shoots when the birds flew like gnats, at least, that's how we remembered them. Thick as gnats.

Doc saw my kids grow up like a movie made from snapshots flipped under your thumb, one snapshot per year. First, they were two-legged retrievers, then shooters. When we were alone, Doc would tell me, "You're doing the right thing here, bringing the kids."

And he'd grin big at them and make them smile and be glad to be part of this circle of friends.

Seven or eight years ago, Larry switched fields, got us farther out in the country into a long, narrow field with a knoll and a telephone line that cut diagonally across one corner. The tractor couldn't get up to the pole, so pokeberries, goldenrod, and wild blackberries grew head high into a thicket. Doc hunted from this thicket.

The birds would surprise us sometimes, sneaking into the field without a shot being fired, and land on the wire by the pole. Doc never shot a bird off the wire. He'd jump them, shoot, and take his chances. Sometimes just run them to us.

There were better shots in the field than Doc, some young bucks with sweet swings and sharp eyes. But Doc held his own, shot a light twenty-gauge, and had a form that was practiced, consistent, shaped by years of shooting over and over and over. Doc conceded nothing to the young bucks.

Confident. That's what Doc was. Been there before, in any situation. Knew what happened next, like watching a rerun of *Jeopardy* and knowing all the answers. That's where his confidence came from; confident enough to tease or be teased.

One year, the mice must have been scarce or the doves slow, and an assortment of hawks worked the field over before the season started. At least four were regulars, including one red-tail that used to sit in an old white oak across the road and watch us shoot, like we were cutting in on his action.

They'd drift in the risers coming off the hot field in early September, broken only by lazy, intermittent flaps to gain a few feet. When they cruised over the field, the doves would lay low. One opening day, as we quit, we turned back and saw the red-tail zoom low off the ground, daring any doves that had slipped in behind us for feed to spring up. You could tell that this red-tail made a living at it.

The next Monday afternoon, back in the field, Doc dropped a dove in open ground with a bounce. As he started toward it, the red-tail came in low, swooped and grabbed it, and came uphill with the dove. Doc started yelling.

"Get my bird. Get my bird."

The hawk was coming right at me, and I thought of firing a shot in the air to see if I could startle him enough to get him to drop the dove. But in the instant, I changed my mind and watched him flap by.

When we met by the truck at sundown, Doc asked, grinning, "Why didn't you get my bird back?"

The answer was simple: "Doc, if I'd gotten your bird back, I'd never be able to kid you about the hawk stealing it."

Doc laughed as if I'd done the logical thing.

This year, for the first in twenty, Doc didn't show up on opening day. His back had been giving him trouble, an operation had complications. The pool therapy he'd been in to get ready for dove season had gone well to a point, and then he'd had a setback. He wrote Larry a letter explaining it all, wishing us luck. Classic Doc.

Larry suggested we not hunt the pole this year. We all nodded; it only made sense. I watched birds land on the wire and counted them to Doc. Missed hearing the "attaboys" on a good shot, missed calling out birds coming from wherever he wasn't watching. We hunted quietly, thinking between shots of wet-wading trout creeks and doves thick as gnats.

I'm looking for Doc to be back next year on opening day, hunting the pole. To understand that, then you'd have to know Doc.

Kudzu Quail

If you live in the South, you need no introduction to kudzu. For the rest, a brief description or warning may be in order; it's headed your way at the speed of global warming.

Kudzu is an invasive plant species brought from Japan for erosion control. The vines grow about eighteen inches per day and can climb anything. These vines have been known to bring down power lines with their weight. The yard at my first house had a kudzu clump in one corner when I moved in. That winter I pulled the dead vines off to find an apple tree underneath.

Over the years, I've seen abandoned houses and parked highway equipment covered by kudzu. Fields become a mat of vines that hide the topography beneath. Its appetite for growth is bounded only by cold climates.

Many abandoned fields that make good quail habitat also host kudzu. After the first frost, the vines turn brown and brittle. A bird dog running through such a field crackles with each bound and step. A hunter traversing such a field will be convinced that the vines grasp boots with the intention of sending a person headlong into a fall.

Quail in kudzu can be a consternation or a delight and I've had both.

My first bird dog after moving south was a little male Brittany named Clayton. He was registered as white and orange with colored ears and a saddle across his back. His first year mostly was spent on yard work and planted birds, but he quickly became solid on point and retrieved well. Still, we were both new to the quail game and learning as we went.

On one of our early hunts, we had made a round sweep and were heading back toward the house. I lived in a rural area then and we could make quick hunts walking out my back door. This was one of those mornings when we both needed to stretch our legs. The plan was to make a short circle crossing a ridge and some peach orchards, then arrive back in the yard by lunchtime.

On our way was an abandoned homeplace that looked like its owner just gave up and walked away. Honeysuckle had taken over the yard and kudzu owned the field. An old roadbed separated the two. I walked up the roadbed while Clayton bounded through the kudzu, energized by the noise he made with each leap. His ears flopped with every jump and sometimes on his landing he fell into the kudzu and out of sight.

As Clayton checked in near the roadbed, he locked on point. Directly in front of him stood a kudzu lump about waist high. Beyond that, a field of kudzu offered potential quail-holding cover. I moved in ready to shoot and stepped past the clump into the more promising cover behind it.

Nothing flushed.

I stomped the kudzu, backed up and kicked the lump, waited, and kicked it again. Clayton remained locked as solidly as when he first pointed.

As much as I trusted his nose, I had no more ideas. My thought was that a bird or covey may have flushed before we walked up. Perhaps a predator pushed them into the woods. But Clayton never relaxed with any waning of the scent. I gave the lump one more thrashing, waited, then turned to walk away.

As soon as I had turned, the whir of wings spun me around to see a single bird coasting into the trees. If Clayton could have talked, I'd have received a tongue-lashing for not trusting his nose, but he didn't say a word. He was good that way.

On another trip, my hunting partner Gerall and I had three dogs on the ground. His two setters, Rudolph and Amy, were wide-ranging dogs that held a point well. Rudolph was a large setter, white with black markings and a classic pointing style with nose to the birds and tail straight behind. Amy was smaller, white with brown markings. When she was on point, she crouched to the ground and often disappeared when pointing in cover. Clayton ran tighter circuits than the setters and rarely lost dead birds. They were a good trio.

Late in the season, you sometimes get days that feel more like spring than winter, so you cherish these hunts knowing the season will soon end. By midmorning, your sleeves are rolled up and your pace becomes more of a stroll.

Topping a knoll, we looked down as the dogs ran a grassy field toward a washed-out gully. The gully lay beneath enough kudzu to appear level with the banks, but if you stepped in you would drop at least eight feet. This kudzu patch was doing its original job when imported from

Japan, slowing the erosion where heavy rains cut into the banks and took sediment downstream. The vines were woven tightly, holding the banks in place.

Rudolph was the first dog to the gully, locking on point with his nose straight down over the edge. Amy and Clayton backed, seeing Rudolph and seeming to have a favorable whiff themselves.

Gerall and I eased to the top of the gully and assessed our opportunity. If birds flushed, we'd have open shots in any direction, a rare thing on late-season birds.

Stepping up past the dogs, Gerall gave the kudzu vines a rattling kick and we heard birds moving.

When they began to flush, the quail had to fight their way up through the vines. It gave us early warning of their exit and by the rustling we knew the covey had numbers.

The first ones broke out in twos and threes, struggling to get clear, providing time to shoulder our guns and aim. The remainder came out as if paced to give us time to recover from the first shots. Birds dropped and dogs began to retrieve. We stopped shooting to let the last birds escape, wanting to leave enough to maintain the covey. Still, it was a shoot that rarely comes in late winter. Although the kudzu gave the birds cover from hawks, it tied their wings when they had to fly.

The kudzu cover probably worked in the quail's favor most times. Harder to walk through than soybeans, the kudzu fields convinced many hunters to skirt the edges of large, rough patches where the vines tripped them up and hid the potholes beneath. Singles and coveys could hide and let them pass.

When a hard frost glazes dead kudzu vines and makes them crunchy, I can almost hear a little Brittany bounding through with sheer joy from the noise he's making. The ears flop with each leap and sometimes on landing all that pops up is a head checking on my location, and then he leaps again. It's that single bird in a kudzu lump I remember most, however, and the dog that trusted me more than I trusted him.

Hunting the Hurricane

Hurricane Irma lined up in the Atlantic with the southeast coast in her sights. The meteorologists, with days to plan, threw tracking maps on the screen like spaghetti slung by a three-year-old. Initially, Irma targeted the Carolinas and brought back reminders of Hurricane Hugo, which had ripped straight through the heart of the state snapping pines and flooding homes. Then she turned.

Even just twenty-four hours before making landfall, Irma was supposed to go up the east side of Florida and land on Charleston. Water disappeared from grocery stores faster than kids at chore time. Gas prices that had jumped fifty cents per gallon with Hurricane Harvey inched higher.

Gulf Coast residents spoke optimistically about riding it out. One acquaintance posted on Facebook that she and her husband, who live on a boat, planned to stay on the water. They couldn't be persuaded otherwise by friends. Then Irma shifted west.

This meant the track would run up the Gulf Coast of Florida, hit Georgia and veer northwest. Suddenly, the call was for Irma to mostly miss the Carolinas. We breathed a sigh of relief and a prayer for the less fortunate, knowing full well it could shift again.

An e-mail came suggesting we hunt doves the day before the rain bands would hit. Temperatures would be cool to help the dogs. The winds would blow to help the birds and expand the hunters' vocabularies, particularly the expletives.

By the time I left home the morning of the hunt, Irma had hit the Florida Keys at Category Five. Power was lost on the islands as was most communication. As I drove, she bore down on Marco Island and Naples, making a second landfall at Category Four. The people who planned to float through the storm in the Gulf and couldn't be persuaded otherwise by their friends thought better of it, persuaded by wind forecasts of

130 miles per hour. They found refuge on land. Still, the boat stayed on the water.

Once we reached the field, we were distributed to stands under a gray sky. Clouds thickened and, unlike during the total eclipse weeks before, you could easily look at the sun. It had an eggshell color through the clouds that swirled in front of it.

The kids and dogs were assigned stands over in the main field, where adults could supervise, and fences could hem them in. My son and I were dropped off in a hayfield that had just been cut and baled. It was surrounded by clear-cut timber where the ground was covered by gray slash unfortunately the color of doves. Any bird on the ground would be hard to find. Before I could load my pump, my son's first bird had hit the ground.

My stand was down the hill in a depression that caused the horizon to be high. Trees along the edge of the field provided good camouflage to any bird that dropped in and flew low. They could dart almost to my bale before they were silhouetted against gray sky. Then, if I was lucky enough to see the bird, I got a shot.

When the wind gusted hardest, the birds flew best. They seemed to be looking for an evening feed and our field lay between the grainfield and their roost. When low birds got up high enough to shoot, the tail-wind caught them, and we tested our reflexes.

Florida residents kept losing power as the day went on. By late after-noon, Irma was aiming at Tampa. Naples had taken the brunt of it; now Irma slowed and lost energy over land. The waters retreated from the beach, drawn out by the wind on the back of the storm. The only prob-lem was that after the rain fell and the storm passed, it would return with a surge.

As birds flew and fell, they often had enough speed to make the clear-cut. We found ourselves climbing through brush piles, looking in nooks and crannies, and following feathers. At one point, one of our hunters was making the rounds to check on everyone with his Lab, Chester, on the front seat. We put Chester to work in the clear-cut and saved one casualty from the foxes.

Halfway through the hunt, the farmer who cut the hayfield began picking up bales. He had heard that four inches of rain was expected and was afraid his tractor wouldn't be able to navigate the field and the bales would sink in the mud. I assured him his task was more important than mine and he agreed to pick up my bale last.

Birds of all kinds had now taken to the air and were beginning to feed. I heard a killdeer whistling and watched a hawk cruise the clear-cut. No doubt he would eat well tonight. Buzzards soared without a wing beat. Doves slipped into flocks of finches as if trying to sneak through. It almost worked.

I might get away with bragging about my shooting at this point, as I had only one witness and he was family. Perhaps a craft beer is all it would take to secure his testimony. Truth is, hard shots were easy and easy shots were hard. When a bird with a tailwind blasted through the field, it kept a steady speed, and a smooth swing would drop it. But then, a straight-in bird could get almost in range, see the shooter, and use the tailwind to make a cut that would leave LeBron James looking for his shoelaces. It was a good afternoon for humility to hold pride in check.

The darkening skies brought the hunt to an early end. Birds had begun to roost, while hunters began picking up empty shells and gear. The ATV made its round gathering up stragglers and giving retrievers one last chance at downed birds. Back at the truck, hunters used tailgates to line up doves for dressing. Kids and dogs bounded with more energy than the hunters had left. Talk of the next hunt began.

South of us, Florida had over ten million people without power. Over 60 percent of the gas stations in Miami, Gainesville, and Fort Lauderdale were without fuel to sell. The storm surge had yet to hit, and they braced for it. Coastal flooding was beginning in Savannah and Charleston. Downed trees blocked streets, looters were being arrested, and first responders were entering evacuated areas. Utility crews traveled from as far as Michigan to help restore power.

In the morning, my friends in the Gulf posted that they were fine and the boat they live on rode out the storm without damage. Unlike some others, they have a home to go back to.

The dove field is now under heavy bands of rain driven by gusts up to fifty miles per hour. Who knows how far the birds will blow. Hurricane Jose has lined up just north of Irma's path. Some of the early spaghetti noodles track through the Carolinas. With a solar eclipse and a track of lined-up hurricanes, Mother Nature has sent a stern reminder of who is in charge here.

It's been a season when it feels like hurricanes are hunting us. It's nice for a change to hunt a hurricane.

The Christmas Gift

A grizzled old Brittany hobbled onto the gravel road in front of my truck. Just steps behind him, a hunter clambered across the ditch and waved, partly showing appreciation that I was looking out for his dog and partly a suggestion to stop.

I pulled over, always open for a chat with a bird hunter.

"Doing any good?" I asked, looking over the fellow's shoulder and down the hill into a clear-cut. I didn't expect a truthful answer, since coveys are generally guarded more closely than the youngest daughter. That the answer was truthful and emotional caused me to put the truck in park and turn off the engine.

"Got one," he said. "That's all I wanted really." His eyes were misting up. I knew the beginning of a story when I heard it, so I just waited.

"Took the pup to the vet this week for his hips." Even a white-haired dog was still "the pup" to his owner. Time stands still in memories, if not in real life.

"The vet says he's suffering and there's not a lot he can do for him. Says I should put him down. But I've hunted too many times with that pup to just put him down. I had to give him one more."

He couldn't talk for a minute, so I waited. The Brittany had limped over to a sunny spot in the leaves and laid down. He'd probably have trouble getting up once he stiffened.

The fellow continued his story. "I worried that I might have trouble finding a covey close by, one the pup could still hunt for in his shape. But ever since this patch of timber's been cut, a few birds have been here.

"Almost as soon as I let him out, he started acting birdy. If you hunt, you know what I'm talking about. Not only that, he looked younger. His nose and heart were pulling him through that clear-cut even if his legs wouldn't. When we got to the back corner, he pointed."

"The covey must have been busted up, because I flushed just one single bird. It sailed around a holly tree and I was afraid I'd lost it. But I picked it up again around the back side and tumbled it with one shot.

The pup even brought it back to me." His voice trailed off as he repeated, ". . . even brought it back to me."

He needed to tell this story. It seemed part of the ritual—two bird hunters on a gravel road secluded in a national forest. This memory was larger than a single quail and an old bird dog. This gift encompassed us all.

"All I prayed for was one bird and that's what I got," he said. He patted the side of my truck, telling me the story was over. He waved as he turned and walked away.

That story haunts me even now, fifteen years and a couple bird dogs later. The pain of what he had to do was bearable mostly because of what he had done for his pup on that last hunt. It seems to me that anything that takes age off, even temporarily, is a good thing, whether for dog or owner.

Skeet, my Brittany, hunts shorter loops with each passing year. Her muzzle is whitened, and, some mornings, she makes sure I'm coming her way before moving to greet me. I remember the old bird hunter and think maybe he was onto something. Maybe there's no greater gift to a bird dog than birds.

I have no clear-cut, however, where a covey always hangs out. I've tried short loops through old farms where we used to find birds. But Skeet's legs always fade before we find them, if they're still there.

So when Christmas approached, I hatched a scheme to give my Brittany birds for Christmas. The local sportsman's club was glad to oblige, and I booked a double handful of birds and a field for the day after Christmas. To ice the deal, I took my son, Stu, home from college for the holidays, to be my shooter.

The weather cooperated mostly, a bluebird day a touch on the warm side for an old dog running. Skeet bounded out of the truck expecting no more than a run in a field of broomstraw. The first birds surprised her and she bumped them into flight. Stu dropped the last one up and Skeet hunted the dead bird.

I could embellish the afternoon and the bird-hunting prowess of my Brittany, but I'd be lying. She's never been on enough birds to be a great dog and she suffers from being owned by a fellow who lacks enough bird smarts to make her a great dog. None of that matters much when Skeet's on point, however, and my son is kicking up a bird.

Bird hunting is one of those areas where you should never judge yourself or your dog too harshly. Kids play basketball without being reminded they weren't NBA material. Bird dogs deserve the same chance.

Skeet hunted like the family pet she is, sometimes rusty, sometimes solid, never flashy. All that mattered on this bluebird day was that she was my dog pointing birds for my son.

By the time we started looking for singles in the woods, age and lack of conditioning had curbed Skeet's rambunctiousness. In some ways, she hunted better slow, tiptoeing after running birds. Not knowing whether she was breaking point or checking up on runners, I teetered between overhandling and indecision. Finally, age and lack of conditioning had also curbed my rambunctiousness and I just let the dog and the son hunt.

Coming around on the second bunch of birds, both had the routine down. Skeet picked up the scent crossing the field, a light breeze had begun to sweep waves through the broomstraw. Stu approached from the uphill side and knew what to expect as he walked up the birds. His game bag began to have some weight, and being the only youngster in the field, his enthusiasm grew.

Bird hunters build libraries of memories, and you rarely need a card to check them out. Mostly, you can just ask. Or nudge them with a phrase or a landmark that jogs their memories.

Memories like that one are shared gifts and we were creating a new one today.

Skeet started acting birdy in the middle of the field, zigzagging and trying to pinpoint the smell that drove her. She sailed over into a patch of briars and for a moment age released her.

For a moment. After a couple hours, her lack of conditioning, too many years, and the heat had taken their toll. We gave Skeet a breather before we went back to mop up the singles.

Resting on the tailgate afterward, I thought about this Christmas gift. Skeet had more hunting today than an old dog could rightfully pack into a season. Stu saw the family pet in a new light, as if she led double-lives and he'd only just seen the second one. And I have the memory of them both.

Maybe that's what the old hunter was doing all those years ago. He had stopped the hand of time long enough to capture a memory.

This hunt wasn't just for an old Brittany who needed a few more points or a young hunter who shot a handful of birds. This gift was about what was right for a pup, a young hunter, and his dad. Somehow, this gift included an old hunter on a gravel road years ago with mist in his eyes as he told a stranger his story.

This gift encompassed us all.

Winders

Rudolph, a boxy-headed black-and-white setter, bounded over the lip of a bank and disappeared. Amy, his opposite, floated past, crossing Rudolph's trail at an angle to the bank running the contour. She was a wisp of Rudolph in size and weight and appeared to run without effort. My Brittany, Clayton, bounced off to the left, ears flopping and nose popping as he caught wind of songbirds. Gerall and I followed the dogs.

Gerall was twice my age when I met him. After leaving the navy, he married and went to work in a textile plant on the cutting table. Back then, they manually slit fabric on a long table. He and another fellow walked a long slitting knife back and forth the length of that table, cutting cloth all day long. Even into his sixties, that gentleman could walk like he was still pulling knives on the textile table. For him, a quail hunt was a morning stroll.

Every Saturday during hunting season, we turned the dogs loose and just started walking. Having lived in the community all his life, Gerall had access to every peach orchard, soybean field, and old homeplace in the area. Rarely did we have to load the dogs in my truck to go hunt.

On this Saturday morning, we were discussing quail scents and how dogs smell. Mostly I listened. A fellow who has followed dogs for a few decades earned a degree of sorts on the subject, though even for him mysteries remained.

"Dogs aren't all alike," he said, glancing down the hill the way the dogs went. "Take Rudolph. Being the big dog that he is, he runs with his nose to the ground. He finds where the birds were and follows them. Amy reminds me of an old setter bitch I used to own named Missy. She ran with her head up in the air and found where the birds were at that moment. She smelled them on the wind. I'll take a good winder any day. Missy was the best dog I ever owned."

This distinction had some time to sink in, as the conversation stopped when we realized neither of us had seen Rudolph for a while.

I stepped to the rim of the bank and looked down the slope. Amy was circling back and we both spotted Rudolph at the same time. He was down in the gully on point, stylish and rigid, tail straight and a front leg cocked. Amy lay down, honoring the big dog's point.

We edged up on either side, my Brittany honoring the point from the back. The gully opened into a flat bottom in the woods, so if the quail had run out the end they could be anywhere. To the left, the cover consisted mostly of fallen pines, with not much on the ground. Down and to the right of the gully, a honeysuckle patch grew up to the edge of a hardwood stand. To go in there, the birds would be running over open ground.

We stepped up to see what flushed. I guessed on the honeysuckle patch as their hold and was right. My Browning pump was halfway up when they exploded through the trees like they had done this before. I picked a gap on the right of a white oak, followed a bird into it and fired. Moments later, Clayton trotted back to me with a bobwhite held gingerly in his mouth.

As our circle brought us back to the house with some time left in the morning, Gerall suggested we make a pass over by the river, a five-minute drive. We hadn't hunted the marsh along the edge where birds often held when pressure pushed them out of the fields.

I dropped the tailgate on the old Ford and Amy and Clayton bounded in. Rudolph jumped up on the hood, took one more leap to the top, and dropped into the bed from above. Muddy paw prints marked his trail behind him.

For a short drive like this, the dogs did fine in the back, but I tilted the mirror to watch them just the same. They stood for the ride, swaying with the curves, but otherwise steady.

Going down the hill to the river, on my left was an uncut hayfield and on the right a patch of briars kind to neither man nor dog. Both could spend an hour trying to pass through and come out the back side bloody. Briars like these grow more than head high and when pushed from below whip back into your face. About the only way through is to turn your back, push, and take your medicine. Of course, it's hard to shoot plowing backward.

As we drove down along the hayfield, I had one eye on the road and one on the dogs in the mirror. I noticed Amy go stiff, like she had pointed briefly, and then relax. I mentioned it to Gerall.

"Pull off down there," he said, pointing to a pullout where tractors entered the field. As soon as I stopped, the two setters sailed over the side of the truck bed and were tiptoeing up the shoulder, Amy leading the way. I quietly dropped the tailgate for the Brittany and he followed.

"Where'd Amy point?" whispered Gerall. I raised an arm to show him the spot and she was already there, lying on point as she often did, with Rudolph and Clayton lined up behind her.

We approached from the road side of the dogs, hoping to push the birds away from the briars and into the hayfield. Good plans sometimes just fail. The covey broke from the edge of the hayfield and flew straight into our faces. We both swung and shot, though I'll admit missing didn't upset me much. I didn't cherish the torture of looking for birds in a briar patch even Br'er Rabbit would have refused.

After we got the dogs headed toward the river, I asked Gerall, "How did you know?"

He grinned his big grin and laughed. "Just a hunch. Remember what I said about ol' Missy? The winder? I saw her do the same thing once . . . point from a moving truck . . . But people never believed me. Now you've seen it, too."

I don't tell that story much, except in the company of old bird hunters, and usually late at night when a little sipping whiskey has set aside their disbelief. They usually nod and let it soak in, too polite or indisposed to call me a liar.

Say what you want about bird dogs, but from that day forward, I treated every point Amy made as if she'd never lead me astray. Rudolph may point a cold trail and the Brittany may lock down on a songbird until he's discovered his mistake and gone back to hunting. But a dog that points from a moving truck bed earned my trust once I realized that Amy was a winder.

An Old Red Shirt

In my closet hangs an old red shirt. Dusty, faded, and too small, I cannot bring myself to tuck it into the Goodwill bag, not with the pockets full of memories.

Some thirty-odd years ago, my wife and I moved south into a rural area where our neighbors, with one exception, lived beyond the peach orchards surrounding us. Across the road lived a couple who taught us the meaning of hospitality and adopted us. It didn't hurt that the Southern gentleman happened to own two English setters. One was a black-and-white male with a boxy head and a classic pointing style. The female was a wisp of white and speckles who lay on the ground when she pointed. I bought the red shirt so I would show up in a quail field.

The shirt was made of chamois and was warm enough early in the season to hunt in without a coat. Not wanting to depend entirely on my neighbor's setters, that year I bought a Brittany pup and got him started. A feisty little dog, he took nothing off the bigger dogs and over the years retrieved more than his share of the birds. White dog hairs, fine as fly tippet, probably still nestle in the bottom of my shirt pockets, the result of wrestling with him after a good day's hunt.

The Brittany learned quickly hunting with the mature dogs. Sure, he got plenty of yard work before joining the hunting party, but soon became steady enough to come along. To his credit, he naturally seemed to honor a point.

Not long into his first season, I was hunting with him alone one morning in a swampy area full of honeysuckle. The quail found hiding spots like this after being hunted some and the Brittany had trailed them in from the soybean field above.

My Brittany had a fine nose and could follow the scent over and around puddles. I'd watch him start to point, and then ease off like he was melting with the fading scent of running birds.

I caught movement to my left and saw the scuttling covey doubling back on us. Good dog work sometimes takes precedent over good shooting, so I waited and watched. Soon, the pup had picked up the runners, made the U-turn, and passed me heading back.

The covey ran another hundred yards before finding honeysuckle sufficiently thick to hold them. At one corner, the Brittany froze solid enough to pick up by a hind leg and I stepped in beside him. A quick scan showed me one good flight path for escape, so I was a step ahead when the covey broke. I squeezed off on the first bird through the gap and it folded in a flurry of feathers.

After a couple more coveys, I'd had enough and the dog was winded. At home, we posed in the backyard for a photo, shotgun across my knee, quail lined up out front, a Brittany with one eye on the birds as if they might escape, and me in my red shirt.

The Southern gentleman and I hunted for about ten seasons together. Just before he was diagnosed with cancer, I noticed a stiffness about him in the field. His old male setter had reached an age where he slept a lot and ran less than his intentions. So, we were breaking in a new setter pup that came of age late in the season.

Sometimes, late in the quail season, you would get a bluebird day and the ground would smell like plowed soil. We had already started giving small coveys a pass, believing they needed seven or eight birds to be strong the next year. With his three setters and my Brittany, we had no shortage of dogs to beat the bush, so he and I strolled, talked, and tried to keep up with their whereabouts.

I remember a story he once told me of a vision he'd had. He admitted to being a hellion going into the navy and had come out, married, and gone to work in the mill. He'd begun the story by pointing at an old homeplace and told me that's where he'd stood and about the setter that he'd had back then that ran with her head up checking the wind rather than running with her nose to the ground. As his setter had gone into a pine thicket, he said that was when it happened. His deceased mother had appeared to him, real as life. What she said he would never share. But he joined the local Baptist church, was baptized, and became a deacon. He was the sort of man you wanted to point to and tell your son to be like him.

As we walked over a broomstraw knoll looking for our wayward dogs, a scene off a calendar unfolded before us. Golden broomstraw waved against that bluebird sky, and at the bottom of the knoll, the old, speckled female lay down on point. A step back, the old male pointed from the side, and five yards farther back, my Brittany honored. Behind him, the setter pup honored his point. We stopped and admired the scene as if painting it into memory, but not daring to dally long enough for a pup to get impatient.

The covey broke in an explosion, having been held in light cover by mature dogs who knew not to bump late-season quail. Just as I remember that point, I recall seeing my partner swinging his little Remington twenty-gauge and the birds fall before us. He must have had a similar view of me, contrasting against that blue sky in a bright-red shirt.

We lost my friend to cancer not long after that trip and his setters not long after him. My wife and I had already started a family and the first to come along was a blonde-haired daughter with eyes so dark you could barely distinguish the pupils. As a newborn, her hair had been fine and translucent and stood straight out from her head.

After a few months, she had a habit of getting colic and we'd figured out that the best remedy was to warm her up. One evening in November, I remember the moon was full, she came down with it again. I'd been splitting oak for the fireplace and still wore the red shirt. Knowing the chamois would be soft as a baby blanket, I unbuttoned the top buttons and slid her inside my shirt with just her head poking out.

We walked out to the screened porch, and I lay down in the hammock to warm her from my body heat and rock her to sleep. Her discomfort was passing when the moon rose over the pines, and I could see her dark eyes follow it. Minutes later, a coonhound bayed, followed by another, and we got to listen to a race through the woods behind the house.

Dog lovers admit the music of blueticks and redbones has no equal; my daughter and I listened to a symphony, both of us snug inside an old red shirt. I can still see the moonlight dancing off a tuft of golden hair, her dark eyes wide, trying to see what was making such a melody.

That old shirt has outlasted hunting buddies and dogs alike. After the quail got scarce, it ended up in a hall closet, constantly being pushed to the back by coats hung in a hurry. I found it again today as I sorted through warm clothes to donate to people who might need a good coat. I checked the pockets of the shirt, but found only memories of old hunters with visions, bird dogs on point, and a fluffy-haired infant who liked the music of coonhounds.

She's grown now, a son on the way, and she has hunting dogs of her own. With the quail all but gone, she switched to a yellow Lab who has guarded her since he was a pup. He keeps company with her husband's golden retriever, who likes to climb round bales in the dove field.

These days I think sometimes about her inheritance and wonder whether I left the right things behind. With her love of fly rods and Labs, I think maybe I did. And it reassures me, now that I know what to do with that pocket full of memories.

In my grandson's closet hangs an old red shirt.

———

THE END

ACKNOWLEDGMENTS

Jim Casada is one of our finest outdoor scribes. If you have read any of his books you will know that he writes with eloquence and a vocabulary as rich as his Smoky Mountain upbringing. I greatly appreciate him contributing the foreward to this book.

I have long enjoyed seeing the artwork of Bob White in magazines and outdoor books. His ability to bring feeling to the image helps the viewer relate to the content. I thank him for doing that as well with the illustrations in this book.

The Jon Boat Years would never have made it into print without the help of Aurora Bell and others at the University of South Carolina Press. This is my second book published by them and their attention to quality shows in both books.

Good editors make writers better. I have been blessed to work with some of the best. My longest writing relationship has been with the editors at *South Carolina Wildlife Magazine*, starting with John Davis and Linda Renshaw, and now with Joey Frazier. All were fine friends and editors.

I have also written for *In-Fisherman* magazine for quite a while. Doug Stange has been the editor throughout that time, joined later by Rob Neumann. Both have helped polish my writing and for that I am grateful.

The editors at *Gray's Sporting Journal* have also been among the best I have worked with and it would be hard to single out any one.

A number of the stories in this book have appeared in magazines previously, though the versions may differ.

"If a Tree Falls," "My Buddy's Fishing Hole," "Hunting with KP," "A Class in Ethics," "Blurred Memories," "Hunting the Pole," "Coldcocked," and "An Old Red Shirt" previously ran in *Gray's Sporting Journal*.

"Another Letter to a Grandson," "A Letter to a Granddaughter," "Your Day Will Come," "The Jon Boat Years," "The Seabee Jacket," and "Old Guys in a Boat" were published earlier in *In-Fisherman* magazine.

"After Dark," "Hunting in a Haunted House," "Pondering Deer Stuff," "A Quack's Guide to Duck Calls," "Reasons for Owning a Dog," "Hunting the Hurricane," and "The Christmas Gift" were published in *South Carolina Wildlife* magazine.

"Yellow Damn Jackets," "Carpy Diem," "Stir Crazy," and "Into the Backing" were published in *American Angler*.

"Fishing Directions," "My Steel Shot Rusted," and "Custer's Last Deer Stand" were also published in *Great Days Outdoors*.

"Low Expectations" previously appeared in *Fly Fisherman* magazine.

"How to Name Your Turkey," "The Turkey Chainsaw Massacre," and "Growing Your Gobbler" appeared previously in *Wheelin' Sportsman*.

ABOUT THE AUTHOR

Jim Mize writes humor and nostalgia about his escapades chasing fish with a fly rod or occasionally waving a shotgun barrel at upland birds. He has had the good fortune to pursue fish in far-flung places such as Scotland and New Zealand, as well as across the Rocky and Appalachian Mountains. His articles have appeared in *Gray's Sporting Journal*, *Field & Stream*, *South Carolina Wildlife*, *In-Fisherman*, *Great Days Outdoors*, and other magazines. His stories and books have been selected for over eighty Excellence In Craft awards, including the Pinnacle Award, the highest award for books from the Professional Outdoor Media Association. His previous books include *The Winter of Our Discount Tent*, *A Creek Trickles Through It*, *Hunting With Beanpole*, and *Fishing With Beanpole*. Jim writes from his cabin in the South Carolina mountains while his Lab, Moose, keeps the bears at bay.